D0982545

More Tales from the Tribe Dugout

Russell Schneider

www.SportsPublishingLLC.com

ISBN: 1-58261-680-9

Publishers: Peter L. Bannon and Joseph Bannon Sr.
Senior managing editor: Susan M. Moyer
Acquisitions editor: Mike Pearson
Developmental editor: Elisa Bock Laird
Art director: K. Jeffrey Higgerson
Dust jacket design: Heidi Norsen
Project manager: Jim Henehan
Imaging: Heidi Norsen
Photo editor: Erin Linden-Levy
Vice president of sales and marketing: Kevin King
Media and promotions managers: Kelley Brown (regional),
        Randy Fouts (national), Maurey Williamson (print)

Printed in United States of America

Sports Publishing L.L.C.
804 North Neil Street
Champaign, IL 61820

Phone: 1-877-424-2665
Fax: 217-363-2073
Web site: www.SportsPublishingLLC.com

This book is dedicated to many, beginning again with my wife and best friend (and primary editor-proof reader-adviser) Catherine, whose support and encouragement over the years have been a blessing and, as with my previous 10 books, deservedly shares whatever success *More Tales from the Tribe Dugout* achieves …

And to my late mother, Maybelle, the greatest and most unwavering Tribe fan I ever knew, and to my late father, Robert, who eventually came to appreciate baseball because his wife and son were so completely addicted to and so in love with the game …

And to the players, managers, coaches, and executives of the Indians whose tales are related on the following pages …

And to baseball itself, a most wonderful game that has survived so much from within its ranks, as without, a game that was described by the late Red Smith as "being dull only to dull minds" …

And to the fans who love baseball and especially the Indians.

—*Russell Schneider*

Contents

Acknowledgments

There are many whose assistance and cooperation I gratefully acknowledge in the preparation and development of *More Tales from the Tribe Dugout;* as well as those who helped make my career as a sportswriter truly a labor of love—after I became painfully aware that writing about sports would be easier than trying to hit a baseball as a minor league catcher—beginning at the beginning with Gordon Cobbledick, the late sports editor of *The Plain Dealer*, who hired me in 1964 to cover the Cleveland Indians; his successor and my friend and mentor, Hal Lebovitz; other colleagues and competitors during and since those great (and sometimes not-so-great) days covering the Tribe and then the Cleveland Browns, including Chuck Heaton, Bob August, Hank Kozloski, Bob Sudyk, and the late Jim Schlemmer; current Tribe beat writers Paul Hoynes and Burt Graeff of *The Plain Dealer*, Jim Ingraham of the *Lake County News-Herald* and *Lorain Journal*, and Sheldon Ocker of the *Akron Beacon-Journal*, who repeated to me some of the anecdotes and stories that appear in the following pages; certainly (most) past and present members of the Indians; and Mike Pearson of Sports Publishing L.L.C., who presented the opportunity for this book and others of mine to be written and published, and Elisa Bock Laird of Sports Publishing L.L.C. for her editorial contributions. Thanks again.

—*Russell Schneider*

Introduction

I t's a refrain heard throughout baseball (with some exceptions, most notably in New York and possibly lately in Atlanta). But in few other major league cities is it more appropriate than in Cleveland, where the Indians have teased and frustrated us through most of the team's existence.

That is: *Wait until next year.*

And sadly, for those of us always forgiving fans of the Tribe, next year arrived only twice in the 104 years since the franchise became a charter member of the American League in 1901.

Those two glorious occasions occurred in 1920, when the Indians beat the then-Brooklyn Robins in the World Series, and in 1948 when they vanquished the then-Boston Braves for a second world championship.

Imagine! In the 56 seasons since the Indians were acknowledged to be the best team in baseball, Harry Truman was in the White House, the Cleveland Browns won their third straight championship in the All-America Football Conference, Philadelphia defeated the then-Chicago Cardinals for the National Football League title, and golfer Ben Hogan won the U.S. Open.

Even more sadly, in the 19 years before the Indians prevailed in 1920 and since they won baseball's greatest prize in 1948, it seems we've often been taunted and tormented with false hope.

There can be no doubt that being an Indians fan requires an act of sheer faith.

The Indians came close to fulfilling our hopes by winning three more pennants before failing in the World Series, once miserably and twice with heart-breaking cruelty. They were swept by the then-New York Giants in 1954, then lost to the Atlanta Braves in six games in 1995, and finally bowed out to the five-year-old Florida Marlins in the 11th inning of the seventh game in 1997.

Of course, there were other seasons that appeared promising, when the Indians almost won. But again they fell short for one reason or another and more than anything prolonged—even worsened—our frustration. It happened most recently during the so-called "Era of Champions" (as designated by the publicity department) from 1994 to 2001, when the Tribe won six division championships but lost four times in playoffs for the pennant.

Still, despite their shortcomings on the field, the Indians had and have their share of interesting personalities—OK, even *characters*—whose anecdotes and antics off the field generated interest, even when the games produced more tears than cheers.

All of which provided the genesis of this book, *More Tales from the Tribe Dugout*, as they did in the first *Tales from the Tribe Dugout*.

I hope you find them as engaging and entertaining as I did through my years as a reporter covering the Indians and still do as a fan—one who's still waiting until next year.

—*Russell Schneider*
Cleveland, Ohio
October 2004

The Tales

Andy Allanson
(Catcher, 1986-1989)

After he was selected by the Indians as their second choice in the 1983 amateur draft and was named the catcher on the major league All-Rookie team in 1986, Andy Allanson's career quickly careened down hill. At the end, it consisted of 512 games over parts of eight seasons with five teams, including Detroit, Milwaukee, San Francisco, and California, in addition to Cleveland.

The fault might have been that success came too soon for Allanson. After he batted .263 with five homers and 50 RBIs in 133 games in 1988, Allanson became embroiled in a protracted hassle with the Indians on the contract they offered for 1989. He filed for salary arbitration and, to the dismay of Tribe general manager Hank Peters, won a healthy increase.

However, it also cost Allanson his job, which Peters made clear in the wake of the arbitrator's decision favoring the catcher.

When asked what Allanson's future with the Indians would be, Peters replied, "His future is in the past," and when the 1989 season ended, Allanson was released.

Sandy Alomar Jr.
(Catcher, 1990-2000)

Sandy Alomar's primary problem with the Indians was neither hitting nor catching, but staying healthy, which ended his stint in Cleveland. After his eighth trip to the disabled list with another knee injury in 1999, he shrugged and said, "If 50 guys are standing around in a group and somebody throws a bomb, you can bet it'll hit me—only me. That's been the story of my career."

Alomar admitted he cried—although he shed what he called "happy" tears—upon being greeted with a standing ovation by the fans in his return to Jacobs Field as a member of the Chicago White Sox on April 2, 2001.

"It was a very touching, very sentimental time for me, after so many years with the Indians, and going through so many tough times [1990-1994] and then so many very good times [1995-2000]," he said. "I'll always remember being a part of the family of this city."

Max Alvis
(Third baseman, 1962-1969)

After being traded by the Tribe and then retiring from the Milwaukee Brewers in 1970, Max Alvis went to work for a bank in Jasper, Texas, and eventually became its president.

"I guess you can say I got to be president of the bank kind of like the way I learned to play third base. You get enough bad hops, and pretty soon you can handle them. I made enough mistakes at the bank and learned from them, just as I did in baseball."

Tony Amato
(Indians clubhouse manager, 2002-)

Tony Amato's memories of Albert Belle remain vivid—particularly an incident that occurred in 1995.

"A.B. [Belle] complained that it was too cold in the clubhouse and asked me, 'Tony, did you do this? … Did you turn the thermostat down during the game?' I told him I didn't, and he went around the clubhouse asking guys if they did it, but nobody admitted they'd turned it down.

"So he went to his locker, grabbed a bat, and said, 'I'll make sure no one turns it down again,' and smashed the thermostat to pieces. That was it. We all looked at each other, but nobody said anything until A.B. left the room. Then it was like, 'Holy cow!' We couldn't believe what he did."

(In his next paycheck Belle was docked the cost of replacing the thermostat and repairing the damage done to the wall.)

Brian Anderson
(Pitcher, 1996-1997, 2003)

During a spring training bus trip to Vero Beach, Florida, to play Los Angeles in 2003, Brian Anderson suddenly realized he'd forgotten his equipment bag. It meant he had no baseball cleats and no glove, which he needed because he was scheduled to pitch against the Dodgers that day.

"When we got to Vero," he said, "I borrowed a car and went shopping at a Wal-Mart and Champs Sporting Goods store. I bought a glove at Wal-Mart for $24.95 and a pair of spikes at Champs for $65. The glove was beautiful two-tone ready-to-play leather—but it was a softball glove, nothing I would use if I didn't have to."

As it turned out, Anderson ruefully recalled, "Naturally, I got three comebackers that day, although I've got to say, the glove worked fine."

Afterward he gave it away.

• • • • •

"When I was growing up in Geneva, [Ohio], the Indians were the team my family and I always rooted for, always hoped they'd do well. I listened to all their games on the radio, and I'll never forget the time—I was three or four years old—when my sister and I had our pictures taken with Brett Butler. It was at one of those photo days at the old Stadium, and he had each of us on his knees. That was really neat. My mom still has that photo.

"Those were what [the media] call the 'bad old days,' but to me they were good. I mean the players were good. All of them.

"I was very disappointed when the Indians let me get away in the [1997] expansion draft [to Arizona], but it turned out to be a tremendous break for me. The Diamondbacks gave me the ball and gave me the opportunity to pitch, which I probably would not have gotten in Cleveland. In those days if you had a rough outing, they'd send you back to Buffalo and bring up somebody else."

•　•　•　•　•

Anderson returned to the Tribe as a free agent in 2003, but with a record of 9-10 on August 25, he was traded to Kansas City for two minor leaguers and subsequently re-signed with the Royals in 2004.

However, Anderson struggled early in the season and, with a 7.71 earned run average, was demoted by the Royals to the bullpen, after which he was his own severest critic. "Nobody is this bad ... I mean nobody in pro ball," he said. "You could take some kid in rookie ball, give him 10 or 11 starts and he would not do what I've done. Nobody can possibly be this bad—but I am.

"It's no fun being me ... not this season."

Alan Ashby
(Catcher, 1973-1976)

"I often think about our teams of the early 1970s, all the good young players we had and how great it might have been if we could have stayed together longer than we did," Alan Ashby said.

Among them were former teammates Ray Fosse, Rick Manning, Duane Kuiper, Buddy Bell, George Hendrick, Dennis Eckersley, Chris Chambliss, Dick Tidrow, Charlie Spikes, John Lowenstein, and Rick Waits, along with veterans Gaylord Perry and Frank Robinson, who took over as Tribe manager in 1975.

During Ashby's four seasons in Cleveland the Indians finished above .500 only once, 81-78 in 1976, but as he pointed out, "A lot of the guys we had back then went on to have good careers with other teams.

"We also had some guys who are now talking good games."

The former players turned broadcasters are Kuiper for the San Francisco Giants, Fosse for the Oakland Athletics, Manning for the Indians, Lowenstein, a former radio and television "voice" of the Baltimore Orioles, and Ashby for the Houston Astros.

Ashby has been calling Astros games on the air since 1998 after retiring from a 17-year playing career with the Indians, Toronto, and Houston.

Ken Aspromonte
(Second baseman, 1960-1962; manager, 1972-1974)

"I grew up in Brooklyn in a very tough neighborhood where it was always a dog-eat-dog atmosphere, which probably was the reason I was so hot-tempered as a player," Ken Aspromonte said. "In retrospect, I realize my temper kept me on the bench a lot. I took everything so personally.

"I think I was a pretty good player. ... I had good statistics, especially in the minor leagues, but once I got to the big leagues, I let my temper get the best of me. I started fighting myself. I took everything too personally, which hurt me as a player, especially after I got to the big leagues."

•　•　•　•　•

After a mediocre seven-year playing career with six major league teams and three seasons in the Japanese Central League, Aspromonte managed in the minor leagues for four years. He was hired by Gabe Paul to pilot the Indians in 1972, a job he held for three seasons, compiling an overall won-lost record of 220-260.

Looking back at the time he was fired and replaced by Frank Robinson, who became Major League Baseball's first black manager, Aspromonte said, "Attendance was down and the team was bad. A fall guy was needed, and I was it.

"But I have no regrets about not being in baseball anymore. It probably will mean I'll live a little longer than if I were still in the game."

Bobby Avila
(Second baseman, 1949-1958)

Late in the Indians' pennant-winning season of 1954, when they set an American League record (since broken) by winning 111 games, Bobby Avila was batting in the high .380s and told reporters, "If I hit .375 or better, I will run for president of Mexico."

As it turned out, Avila did neither, although he won the batting championship with a .341 average, was a member of the AL All-Star team, and finished third in the balloting for the Most Valuable Player award.

"I was only kidding about running for president. ... I was not a politician," he said during a recent visit to Cleveland.

But still, after he retired from baseball, Avila served a term as mayor of Vera Cruz, his hometown.

"I was born in Vera Cruz, I grew up in Vera Cruz, I was married in Vera Cruz, I was the mayor of Vera Cruz, and when I die, I will be buried in Vera Cruz," he said.

A few months after attending a reunion of the 1954 Indians in Cleveland, Avila died in Vera Cruz on October 26, 2004, of complications from diabetes. He was 84.

Joe Azcue
(Catcher, 1963-1969)

It was during the "bad old days" of Cleveland baseball that Joe Azcue—a.k.a. the "Immortal Cuban"—played for the Indians and still finds it hard to understand why the team was so bad back then.

"Look at the starting pitchers we had," said Azcue, naming Sam McDowell, Luis Tiant, Sonny Siebert, and Steve Hargan. "We should have won a couple of pennants because nobody in the league had better starters, except we didn't have the middle relievers we needed.

"I'll never forget the time Tiant came up [from Class AAA Portland on July 19, 1964,] and blew away the Yankees [3-0, with a four-hitter, striking out 11]. It was amazing, although I wasn't surprised because I had faced him in Cuba before we both came to the United States, and I knew how good he was."

•   •   •   •   •

"Another game I'll never forget was one that McDowell pitched for us in 1963. [Manager] Birdie Tebbetts called Sam and me into his office before the game and told Sam, 'If you throw anything except a fastball or a change-up, it will cost each of you $100,' which was a lot of money then. We followed Birdie's orders, and Sam shut out the Yankees even though they figured out what was happening—that Sam wasn't going to throw anything but fastballs and change-ups.

"Yogi Berra came up to the plate late in the game and said, 'Geez, Joe, we know what's coming, and we still can't hit it. The kid is too tough.'"

•   •   •   •   •

"When I got traded to Boston in 1969 the guy who was the manager, Dick Williams, told me, 'Look at the way we pitch over here,' like it was something real good. I said to him, 'Damn, you must play with a different kind of ball, or something, huh?' I guess he didn't like the way I said it, because a week passed and I did not play very much. They were using me as mop-up. Not like what they told me when they traded for me.

"[Then] we went to Minnesota and in the last game of the series Williams called me in from the bullpen to pinch hit. I walked all the way to the plate and [umpire] Tom Haller said, 'What are you doing? Hurry up, the beer is getting warm.' I said, 'This is my last game with this team, why should I hurry?' He didn't believe me, but it was.

"I swung three times and went back to the dugout. Williams screamed at me, 'You so and so, that will cost you $100.' I said to him, 'You know what you can do—you can kiss my Cuban ass,' and I put all my stuff in a grocery sack and walked out. He yelled, 'You cannot walk out on us, you cannot quit,' and I said, 'Watch me. Watch the door hit my ass,' and I did. I walked out.

"I called my wife to come and pick me up and we drove back to Overland Park, [Kansas]. That was some-time in May. Then my phone started to ring. The reporters in Boston called me. Lots of people called me. Other teams, too. They wanted to know if something was wrong with me. I said no, not with me, with Williams. I said I wouldn't play for that guy. All they wrote in Boston was that I was hard to handle, stuff like that. Finally they made a deal for me with California for Tom Satriano.

"When I got to Boston with the Angels, all the fans booed me, worst I ever was booed. But I just smiled and doffed my hat and then they liked me again. They started clapping their hands. But Williams never said anything to me, and I didn't say anything to him. He was still pissed off at me, and I was still pissed off at him.

"But then, 30-some years later I was at one of those old-timers games and so was Williams. When he saw me

Carlos Baerga dives to tag Ryan Klesko for the second out of a double play. Baerga was beloved in Cleveland for his fearlessness in the field and at the plate. Otto Greule Jr./Getty Images

he asked, 'Hey, are you still a grouch?' and I said to him, 'My God, get a life,' and then I called him a name, but he didn't hear that part, which was a good thing."

Carlos Baerga
(Second and third baseman, 1990-1996, 1999)

"I was shocked when the Indians traded me [on July 29, 1996], but it probably was the best thing that ever happened to me because I became a Christian after leaving Cleveland," Carlos Baerga said. (His free-wheeling lifestyle was the reason he was dealt to the New York Mets.)

And, just as the trade initially upset Baerga, Tribe fans also were outspokenly angered by the deal. The day after it was made an airplane circled Jacobs Field pulling a banner that read, "Trade [John] Hart, Not Baerga."

One of the reasons they hated to see Baerga leave was best elicited in a comment by longtime play-by-play announcer and former pitcher Herb Score, who once said about Baerga: "He's fearless. If a freight train were bearing down on him [at second base], I wouldn't be surprised if he'd stay in there and complete the double play."

Danys Baez
(Pitcher, 2001-2003)

Before he was allowed to leave as a free agent to sign with the Tampa Bay Devil Rays, Danys Baez looked back on his career in Cleveland and said, "The toughest hitter I've faced is [Seattle's] Edgar Martinez. He always seemed to be so comfortable at the plate against me. It was like he looked out at me and said, 'Danys Baez … who is he? I'm going to hit this guy, and I don't care how hard he throws the ball or what he throws.'

"And then he did hit me, usually."

Scott Bailes
(Pitcher, 1986-1989)

"One of the biggest thrills of my baseball career was in 1987 when I was on the same pitching staff as two Hall of Famers, Steve Carlton and Phil Niekro," Scott Bailes said. "I tried not to show it … you know, I tried to be real cool around them, but it was hard. Especially after I saved a game for Niekro.

"It was against the Detroit Tigers [on June 1, 1987]. We beat them 9-6, and it gave Phil and his brother Joe the record for the most major league victories [530] by two brothers. Until that game they had lost four or five games in a row, and their families had been flying all over both leagues to be with one of them when he would have won the game that broke the record.

"When I replaced Phil in the eighth inning, he warned me, 'Don't blow this [expletive] game. ... Joe and I have been trying too long to win one.' Afterward Phil autographed one of his gloves, and he also gave me the pair of spikes he wore. I have them in my trophy room at home."

• • • • •

Bailes went on to pitch for California from 1990 to 1992 and retired.

Well, *sort of.*

As he admitted, "I went home to Springfield, Missouri, and didn't touch a baseball, not even to play catch, until the summer of 1996 when I started playing in an over-30 league, pitching and playing some first base. It was just a beer league; we never practiced, just played one night a week, and at the end of the season we spent our own money to go to a tournament in Arizona. We played three games, lost two of them and were eliminated, then played golf for three more days, and went home.

"At the time Dan O'Brien Jr. was the assistant general manager of the Texas Rangers and saw me pitch in the tournament. He called me and said, 'Hey, you're throwing

harder now than you ever did,' and asked if I'd be interest-
ed in playing pro ball again. At first I said no, that I had
gone to the tournament only to be with my buddies and
play some golf with them. He told me, 'Well, if you decide
you have an interest [in making a comeback], call me.'

"When I told my wife and kids about it they encour-
aged me to give it a try. My kids were at the age then where
it was kind of cool for them to know someone in the big
leagues, especially if it was their father, so I called O'Brien
and asked if he was serious. He said he was, and I told him,
'If I try it, I'd need at least a month to work out and get in
shape because I don't want to embarrass myself.'

"He agreed, and I went to winter ball [1996-1997]
and pitched great. I had an ERA of two-something against
a lot of major league hitters and went to spring training
with the Rangers as a non-roster invitee. I had a great
spring training; I think I gave up only one run in 14 or 15
innings and agreed to go to [Class AAA] Oklahoma City
because it was close to home. The wife and kids could
come down to see me and then go home when I went on
the road. I kind of planned to finish the season in Triple A
and enjoy myself and then fade into the sunset as a
washed-up 35-year-old left-hander.

"But in the middle of the [1997] season injuries to a
couple of [Texas] pitchers changed my plans. The Rangers'
plans, too. They called me up, and I had the best three-
month run that I ever had in the big leagues. I was reliev-
ing, pitching the seventh and eighth innings and setting up
for [closer] John Wetteland, and did great. I had a two-
something ERA and made the team again in 1998.

"But then, about three-quarters through the season I got a sore shoulder and the Rangers' doctor started giving me cortisone shots. We were winning and heading into the playoffs, where I'd never been, and I was determined to stay on the roster and go to Yankee Stadium to pitch against New York. So I kept pitching—and getting cortisone—but when we got swept by the Yankees in the first round of the playoffs, that proved to be it for me.

"I had arm surgery to repair a couple of small tears in the rotator cuff that had become major tears, and my biceps tendon also had become detached, and they fixed that, too. I went to spring training in 1999, and although my arm didn't hurt anymore, it was dead. I couldn't throw 70 miles an hour, and it was all over for me.

"But I guess it was a pretty amazing comeback while it lasted. Some PR guy somewhere told me that it was the longest non-injury layoff or retirement from baseball ever in the major leagues, except for during World War I and World War II when guys came back from the service to resume their careers."

Len Barker
(Pitcher, 1979-1983)

"It was really weird, the night I pitched my perfect game [on May 15, 1981]," Len Barker said. "I knew I had good stuff, real good stuff, and what made it so weird is that I had total command, which wasn't always the case with me. That night I could throw anything, any pitch, anywhere I wanted. And even though it was a tight game [Indians 3, Toronto 0], it felt so easy. But I have to admit,

Len Barker celebrates after pitching a perfect game on May 15, 1981—a 3-0 victory over Toronto. Russell Schneider Collection

the possibility of a perfect game didn't enter my mind until the last inning. Honest, it didn't."

Attendance at the Stadium that night was 7,290, but as Barker said, "I've probably signed autographs for about 150,000 fans, and just about all of them said they were at the game, which also was pretty weird."

Gene Bearden
(Pitcher, 1947-1950)

Gene Bearden pitched for the Indians and won (8-3) the playoff game against the Boston Red Sox for the 1948 pennant, which arguably was the single most important victory in the 104-year history of the Cleveland franchise.

But it wasn't Bearden's biggest thrill in baseball.

"Nothing was greater in my mind than pitching my first game," he said. "I'll never forget it. It was in Washington in old Griffith Stadium on May 8, 1948. You know, you work all your life to get to the big leagues, and there I was pitching against Sid Hudson, a real good veteran pitcher, and we won 6-1.

"It was in that game that Larry Doby hit a home run that must have traveled 550 feet, clean out of the park, and if anybody—Mickey Mantle or anybody—ever hit a ball farther, I sure would've liked to see it.

"I don't have any regrets, none whatsoever. I was one of the fortunate few who got to play in the big leagues and one of the even fewer who were fortunate to get into a World Series. I knew what it was like to be on top. Just think how many kids play and play and play baseball but never reach the big leagues.

"No, I was lucky and I don't have a single regret."

Buddy Bell
(Third baseman and outfielder, 1972-1978;
coach, 1994-1995, 2003-)

"It was the start of my major league career, and it should have been one of the best times of my life, but it wasn't. Not at first. It was scary. We didn't know what to do," recalled Buddy Bell about 1972 when he and two fellow rookies, pitcher Dick Tidrow and second baseman

Jack Brohamer, made the team and were heading to Cleveland to open the season.

"The three of us had played at [Class AAA] Wichita in 1971, and you can imagine how excited we were to be in the big leagues. But before we were to go to Cleveland, we played exhibition games en route, after leaving Tucson [spring training], and the last two were in New Orleans against the Chicago Cubs.

"It was right after the first game—I don't remember if we won or lost—that Steve Mingori and Ray Fosse, who were our player representatives, held a meeting and told us that the players association was going on strike. The three of us had no clue as to what it meant for us, but as we found out, we were stuck in New Orleans with about $30 among the three of us and no credit cards.

"What happened was that Hammer's [Brohammer's] dad drove Jack's car over from spring training and then flew back to his home in California, and we started for Cleveland. But to make matters worse, we almost got in a wreck. I was driving, Tidrow was in the passenger seat, and Hammer was in the back, sleeping. It happened near Newport, Kentucky. The car was a [Plymouth] Duster, and the brakes were the kind that, you know, if you pushed on the pedal real hard, the brakes locked up and the car would skid, which is what happened. We wound up doing a 360 in the median [of the freeway]. Fortunately, we didn't hit anything. All of our suitcases fell on top of Hammer in the backseat, but otherwise, we were OK.

"Somehow we made it to my parents' home in Cincinnati before we ran out of money. My mom and dad took us in, and we stayed with them a couple of days, but, being rookies, we still didn't know what to do. Finally, we drove to Cleveland. The strike was still on, so we stayed with friends and waited to see what was going to happen.

"A couple of days later an agreement was reached, and the season started. Graig Nettles was the Indians' third baseman then, and a couple of outfielders got hurt in spring training so [manager] Ken Aspromonte put me in right field, even though I had never played the outfield before that spring. I was scared that I'd screw up, but I never let anybody know. Actually, I told [Aspromonte and the coaches] that I had played some in the outfield because I really wanted to make the team and figured that was my only chance.

"As it turned out, I was OK. The first few games I was a little hesitant, but after that I was fine. My only complaint about playing the outfield is that it gets kind of boring. It's not as intense as it is when you're playing the infield. I even moved over to center field when the Indians traded Del Unser."

●　●　●　●　●

Bell returned to his natural position at third base when Nettles was traded to the New York Yankees on November 27, 1972.

"As every longtime old Tribe fan will remember, the Indians were rebuilding damned near every year," he lamented. "But the truth be told, I wouldn't trade any of those years for anything. They were great seasons—except for that first week when the players association went on strike."

•   •   •   •   •

One of the Tribe's former coaches, Dave Garcia, recalled instructions he received from then-general manager Phil Seghi when Bell was a young third baseman.

"Phil told me," Garcia said, "'I want you to work with Buddy Bell. He catches every ground ball with one hand.' So I hit Buddy about 5,000 grounders the next two days, and then I went to Seghi and said, 'You're right. He does catch everything with one hand—just leave him alone.'"

Which was well said. Bell went on to win six Gold Glove awards as a (sometimes one-handed) third baseman.

Gary Bell
(Pitcher, 1958-1967)

"I admit I had a reputation for being … well, you know, a *fun* guy, loose, a guy who enjoyed himself, but I always worked hard and kept myself in good shape," Gary Bell insisted. "Sure, I'd get [blitzed] sometimes, but I can honestly say I never took a drink the day I pitched. Not ever.

"I also admit I did not have a good relationship with [then owner] Gabe Paul. Sometimes he gave me hell about some things he had no business getting into.

"Once he called me into his office and, with [interim manager] George Strickland there, raked me over the coals. I thought that was pretty horse [expletive]. If he had something to say to me about my personal life, he should have said it to me in private.

"But then again, in those days you were like a kid and got slapped on the bottom when you did something that management didn't like. Times are different now."

• • • • •

Bell also was a central figure in Jim Bouton's 1970 tell-all book, *Ball Four*, about big league shenanigans.

"I thought it was a helluva good book," Bell said, "though a lot of guys took it seriously and were mad at Bouton for writing it. In those days baseball—and the players—were a lot different. It was kind of like Bouton broke an unwritten code by writing about what players did off the field.

"But the way things are nowadays, hell, that book would be lightweight."

• • • • •

"I liked pitching for Birdie [Tebbetts] when he managed the Indians [1963-1966]. He could be pretty tough, but he was a pretty good guy. Sometimes even funny. I remember one night after a game in Los Angeles, there were about eight of us at a restaurant called Googies, right around Pershing Square. We were having breakfast about 2 a.m., and the curfew was midnight.

"We were sitting there eating and, lo and behold, who walks by and looks in the window but Birdie. He came in and started laughing and said, 'Boys, don't get up now. You might as well finish eating because I got you,' and the next day he took our money. I don't remember how much he fined us, but the kind of money we were making in those days—the early 1960s—50 or even 25 bucks was a lot, especially with Gabe running the team.

"I played in Cleveland for nine years, won almost 100 games, and was making 24 grand when I got traded to Boston, which was a little different than it is now, baby. I got a huge bonus when I signed with the Indians—all of four grand. It was better in Boston. The most the Red Sox paid me was 40 grand, but that's nothing compared to what's happening today.

"Oh, to be young again."

Albert Belle
(Outfielder, 1989-1996)

A reporter for the *Arizona Republic* in Phoenix was given an assignment to visit the Scottsdale home of former Indian Albert Belle to ask him his opinion on Sammy Sosa's 2003 use of a corked bat.

Belle, who was caught using a corked bat in 1994, told the reporter, "Isn't it interesting that you and your editor care enough to find my house and ask me about this, but no one cares that I've been taking classes at Arizona State University and that I'm about to get my undergraduate accounting degree."

Ron Belliard
(Second baseman, 2004-)

Through the first month and a half of his first season with the Indians, Ron Belliard seemingly could do nothing wrong at the plate, flirting with a .400 batting average and remaining in the high .300s until midseason.

"Sometimes every ball you hit turns into good luck," he said. "I just go up there and swing the bat. I've been hitting the ball in the right place [on the field]."

And sometimes even on the wrong place of the bat.

"I've never broken so many bats that went for base hits in such a short period before, at least 15 or 20, but that's OK. I'll trade a bat for a hit anytime."

A career .266 hitter in his five previous seasons in the National League, Belliard cooled off as the season wore on but continued to be one of the year's best free agent acquisitions.

Casey Blake
(Third baseman and first baseman, 2003-)

Casey Blake, who sometimes moved from third to first base for defensive purposes in 2003, played first base in his first game in the big leagues in 2000. At the time he was playing for Minnesota in a game against the Indians at Jacobs Field and admittedly did not know all the inner workings of the position.

"I was holding Robbie Alomar on the bag," Blake said, "and he leaned over and whispered, 'Hey, you don't have to hold me. We've got a runner on second base.' When I looked at the Twins' dugout, everybody was laughing, which was pretty embarrassing."

•   •   •   •   •

In 2003, his first season with the Tribe, Blake recalled that his former Twins teammates kidded him after a game in Minnesota.

"I was having a good series, swinging the bat pretty good. After I went five for five in one of the games [Twins third baseman] Corey Koskie, who is a good friend of mine, sent a ball over to our clubhouse for me to autograph. Koskie told our clubhouse manager, 'Tell Casey that I heard he's been telling people in Minneapolis that if he was still with the Twins, he could have a game like that every day and also that he is a much better player [than Koskie], all that kind of stuff.'

"Of course, I never said anything like that, and never would, but Corey wanted to yank my chain, which he did pretty good.

"So I took the ball that Corey sent over and wrote on it, 'To Corey Koskie, I owe it all to you, you are my idol,' and signed it.

"The very next day, after I had the clubhouse manager give it to Koskie, I popped up my first two at bats and went oh-fer [hitless]. After the game Corey said he was tempted to send the ball back, and I was glad he didn't."

• • • • •

Early in the 2004 season, Blake missed three games because of a strained right hamstring.

"I was examined and the doctor discovered that my right leg is slightly longer than the left," he said. "I was told that it might have caused the hamstring problem."

The solution was that a ⅜-inch pad was inserted in the heel of Blake's left shoe. When a reporter facetiously asked if Blake thought the doctor was "pulling his leg," Casey replied, "No, but maybe I should have had him pull my left leg."

Bert Blyleven
(Pitcher, 1981-1985)

Reminiscing about Len Barker's perfect game on May 15, 1981, a 3-0 victory over Toronto, Bert Blyleven said, "There's no doubt in my mind that it was one of the greatest games ever pitched in the history of baseball. I mean the *greatest*.

"Lenny had an outstanding slider that night, and I don't think I've ever seen hitters swinging at balls that looked like they were about belt high and ended up below their knees. He had everything going that night, and I don't think there was a play behind him that anybody could say that it saved the no-hitter. He was awesome.

"From the sixth inning on everybody in the dugout was as nervous as I'm sure he was on the mound, but nobody dared say a word about it being a no-hitter. You know how superstitious ballplayers are. And when he got the last Toronto batter to end the game on a routine fly to Rick Manning in center field, we all leaped to our feet—a couple of guys hit their heads on the ceiling of the dugout, almost knocking themselves out—and we ran out on the field to greet him. I'm surprised we didn't hurt him because, there we were, 24 guys, trying to hug him."

Aaron Boone
(Third baseman, 2004-)

After the Indians signed Aaron Boone to a free agent contract in late June 2004, a story surfaced about the infielder's character. It was told by Hal McCoy, the Hall of

Fame baseball writer for the *Dayton Daily News*, who covered Cincinnati when Boone played for the Reds from 1997 to 2003.

McCoy, the Reds beat writer for 32 years, had suffered optical strokes in both eyes and his vision had been reduced by 50 to 60 percent. The first day of spring training in 2002, McCoy had trouble recognizing the players because he couldn't see well enough. One of them was Boone.

"I was near tears," McCoy said. "Aaron came up to me, and I told him, 'You're seeing me for the last time. I can't see. I'm going to have to quit and go home.'"

Boone asked why, and McCoy explained what had happened to his eyesight.

"Aaron sat me down and said, 'I don't ever want to hear the word quit come out of your mouth again. What's happened to you is no reason to quit something you love doing.'

"I'll never forget what he said … what he did for me that day."

And every day after that in spring training Boone checked with McCoy to see how he was doing.

"He turned me around that day," added McCoy—who is still covering the Reds on a daily basis for the *Dayton Daily News*.

Dick Bosman
(Pitcher, 1973-1975)

Ted Williams was renowned as one of baseball's greatest hitters—perhaps *the greatest* in the game—but Dick

Bosman said he learned more about pitching from Williams than from anyone else.

"Pitching for Williams, when I was a member of the Washington Senators in 1969 and he was our manager, was a very important part of my career," Bosman said. "That season was my first good year in the big leagues, and I give Williams credit for it and also for whatever success I had afterward.

"Because he was such a great hitter, Williams pretty much taught me the art of pitching, however strange that might sound. But think of it. Who should know better than the man who probably was the greatest hitter in the game? It made me a good pitcher then and a good coach now. I owe a great deal to Williams."

Bosman pitched a no-hitter for the Indians against Oakland on July 19, 1974, and hurled three one-hitters when he was with the Senators from 1956 to 1971 (and Texas Rangers in 1972 and part of 1973, after the Washington franchise moved to Dallas). One of those one-hitters was against the Indians in 1969 and was spoiled by Tony Horton, who singled in the second inning. Bosman also pitched a one-hitter in 1970 against Minnesota. He retired as an active player in 1976 after being traded to Oakland.

"I enjoyed my pitching career, but I enjoy coaching even more," Bosman said. "There is something about teaching that really turns me on. When I'm coaching—teaching—the words just come out. I don't always know where they come from, but they're there, and they're right. Many of them from Williams, I'm sure."

Umpire Bill Stewart rules runner Phil Masi of the Boston Braves safe before Lou Boudreau of the Cleveland Indians tagged him during the eighth inning of the World Series in 1948. Hy Peskin/Time Life Pictures/Getty Images

Lou Boudreau
(Shortstop, 1938-1950; manager, 1942-1950)

Before he died in 2001, Lou Boudreau reminisced on his career as a Hall of Fame player, player–manager, and broadcaster—as well as an All-America collegiate basketball player prior to his career in baseball.

"I have only one regret, and it's not that I was born too soon, before the big money came into baseball," he said. "My only regret, after a lifetime in sports, is that my teams won only one pennant [in 1948]. A player's—and a manager's—first World Series is like a child's first taste of ice cream. It's never enough."

Milton Bradley
(Outfielder, 2001-2003)

"I live by a simple creed," said Milton Bradley early in his brief and tempestuous career with the Indians. "If you don't know me and I don't know you, don't approach me and I won't approach you. Don't insult me, and I won't insult you, because you don't know what I will or won't do.

"I want [opposing players] to hate my guts. That way when we beat them and when I get that [big] hit or make that [big] play, it hurts in their soul; it sticks with them and they have trouble sleeping.

"The energy you get when the crowd is booing you and cheering for the pitcher to get you when you're at the plate ... I live for that. Then to be able to get a hit is something special."

•   •   •   •   •

Bradley also expressed disdain for his reputation as a problem player, saying, "I'm the reason why a lot of these people [clubhouse workers and members of the media] have got jobs. I know I am an interesting person. If I wasn't on this team, what would you be writing about?

"I don't just go with the flow. If I believe people are doing things to prove a point or abusing a position of power, I'm not going to sit back and take it. It might seem like I'm acting on the spur of the moment, or emotion, but I know every action has a reaction. I'm willing to accept the consequences to prove a point."

After incurring manager Eric Wedge's wrath for not running out a pop fly in a March 31, 2004, spring training exhibition game and then being suspended for insubordination, Bradley was traded to Los Angeles for two minor leaguers. Upon reporting to the Dodgers, Bradley was quoted as asking God to "bless" Wedge because he "has a lot on his mind." Bradley's antics continued in Los Angeles, where he threw a plastic bottle at Dodgers fans and earned four ejections and two suspensions during the season.

Bobby Bragan
(Manager, 1958)

Recalling his managerial tenure with the Indians, Bobby Bragan said, "I was hired by Hank Greenberg, but shortly thereafter the Indians were sold, and the new owners brought in Frank Lane as the general manager. Knowing Lane and how he operated, I knew I wouldn't be around long—and I was right.

"Midway through the [1958] season we lost a game 2-1 to Boston, on a ninth-inning homer by Ted Williams. When I got into the clubhouse, there was a message from Lane for me to go up to his office. I knew what he wanted. I wasn't a virgin. I'd been fired before.

"Again, I was right. Lane told me, 'Bobby, I don't know how we're going to get along without you, but starting tomorrow we're going to try.' That was it. That's how he fired me."

Ben Broussard
(First baseman, 2002-)

When asked why he takes his guitar on every trip, Ben Broussard replied, "Sometimes when you have a bad day at the park, you can take things in a different direction with the guitar."

Jackie Brown
(Pitcher, 1975-1976)

"Cleveland is a great town, but when I was traded there, I have to admit there was no way I wanted to go," Jackie Brown admitted. "I didn't want to uproot my family, but the big reason why I wasn't sure about going to Cleveland was because of the prominent memory I had of the town. I was there on 'Beer Night' [as a member of the Texas Rangers in 1974] when the fans went crazy and rioted. It was the scariest thing I've ever seen.

"But the last few years [as a major league pitching coach] I could not wait to go back to Cleveland. The new ballpark, the great fans—what a fantastic atmosphere. I'm happy for the people there. After that first bad memory of Cleveland, I found the fans to be just great. I'm glad to have been part of the Indians in a small way."

•   •   •   •   •

On being traded to Montreal for Andre Thornton in 1976: "That sure turned out to be a heck of a deal for Cleveland, so I guess it's fair to say that I did something good for the city and the Indians."

Larry Brown
(Shortstop and second baseman, 1963-1971)

In a 1963 game at the old Stadium in which the Indians beat California 9-5, Larry Brown hit the fourth of four consecutive home runs off Paul Foytack in the sixth inning. Previously, Woodie Held, Pedro Ramos, and Tito Francona delivered homers off the Angels right-hander.

Brown admitted to being—well, *suspicious* when he faced Foytack.

"When I went to the plate, I wasn't even thinking about hitting," he said. "I was getting ready to go down. Instead [Foytack] threw two fastballs down the middle for strikes, and I hit the next one out."

When Foytack was replaced on the mound by Jack Spring, Brown quipped, "They didn't take him out because he gave up four homers. They took him out because he gave up one to me."

(It was one of 47 homers Brown hit in his 12-year major league career with the Indians, Oakland, Baltimore, and Texas.)

•   •   •   •   •

"I also well remember the day that Max Alvis tripped over third base in Chicago [in 1966]. The batter hit the weakest pop-up you ever saw, and, for crying out loud, you could have caught it in your teeth. Maxie went over to get it, stepped in front of the bag, then stepped backwards, tripped, fell, and missed the ball completely.

"I was standing there watching him and later [manager] Birdie Tebbetts said to me, 'Brownie, you've got to catch that ball.' Believe it or not, by gosh, he was serious."

•   •   •   •   •

"I liked Birdie a lot. He was good. One time, when I went back to Cleveland for an old-timers game, I went up to Birdie and thanked him for all he did for me. He said to me, 'Don't thank me. ... I want to thank you. You were the best shortstop I had.'

"I don't know if that was true or not, but I appreciated it a lot."

Dave Burba
(Pitcher, 1998-2001, 2002)

Dave Burba reluctantly recalled one of the longest home runs he ever relinquished.

"It was in 1998, when Charlie Manuel was the hitting coach of the Indians, and I was pitching in a game against the St. Louis Cardinals at Jacobs Field. I threw Mark McGwire a pretty good fastball, and he hit it a ton, a king-sized home run out of the ballpark into the left-field bleachers, away back. It almost went completely out of the park.

"After he hit it, I looked into our dugout and all my teammates were on their feet, looking at where the ball landed—and laughing. I thought to myself, 'Man, that's kind of disrespectful, that my own teammates are dogging me, teasing me.'

"When I went into the dugout at the end of the inning, I was kind of upset about it because even Manuel had a big grin on his face. He was actually giggling. I went up to him and said, 'Dammit, Charlie, what's so funny?' and he said to me, 'Oh, hell, Burb. I just like watching home runs. I don't care who hits 'em. And that one was a beauty.'

"Fortunately, we won the game, so I could laugh about it, too. Not right away, but later."

Ellis Burks
(Outfielder and designated hitter, 2001-2003)

Ellis Burks was the elder statesman among the Indians before he left as a free agent and enjoyed teasing his teammates, especially rookies.

"It was during our first home game in spring training [in 2003] and Ben [Broussard], a young first baseman who's a good kid and a pretty good player, hit a deep fly ball to the gap in left-center field. It was pretty deep and appeared it was going to be a home run, but the center fielder ran and caught the ball just as Ben, who was running with his head down, was making his turn at first base.

"When he approached second base he asked the umpire, 'What happened? Was it a homer?' and the umpire said it was. So Ben went into his home run trot around second and third, and everybody in the dugout wondered what the heck he was doing. We're all saying, 'No, no, noooo.'

"When Ben got home, he jumped on the plate and walked to the dugout with a big smile on his face, and all of us in the dugout started playing tricks on him, giving him high fives and all that, just as if he really had hit a home run.

"Then, all of a sudden, one of the guys said, 'Hey, Dude, it didn't go out,' and Ben said, 'What do you mean? The umpire said it did.'

"Finally Ben realized everybody—even the umpire—was putting him on and got all red faced and embarrassed, and we all laughed again. It was a fun time."

Cy Buynak
(Jacobs Field visiting clubhouse manager)

As the Indians clubhouse manager for 28 years (before switching to the visiting team clubhouse in 1990), Cy Buynak knew virtually everything that was going on behind the scenes with the players of his era.

"Max Alvis usually had a big chew of tobacco in his mouth, and one day during a game he took a grounder off his chest and swallowed his chew. I turned to [then-manager] Alvin Dark in the dugout and said, 'Skip, in a minute we're going to have a problem here.' Alvin asked why, and I told him, 'Because Alvis just swallowed his tobacco, and he's going to come running in here to the john to throw up.'

"With that, somebody on the field called time and Max came running into the dugout, just as I knew he would, and pretended he had to get his sunglasses, or something. Then he threw up.

"All Alvin said was, 'I hope that teaches him a lesson.'"

(It didn't.)

• • • • •

"Bert Blyleven was a great practical joker, but there were times I didn't think he was so funny. He used to pick me up and throw me into one of the big trash cans we kept in the clubhouse," said Buynak, who is slightly more than four feet tall.

"But I usually got even with him. Whenever he'd throw me into trash barrel, the next day I'd tie up his baseball uniform in knots. I guess he knew it was me because, after I did it, he'd come get me and throw me back in the trash can again."

• • • • •

"Probably the funniest guy we ever had on the team was Looie [Luis] Tiant. Everybody tried to pull pranks on him. One time Chuck Hinton put Looie's uniform on, and a reporter from out of town approached him for an interview, thinking he was talking to Tiant. Hinton answered the questions in broken English, and the reporter kept asking him what he was saying.

"I don't think the reporter ever found out that he really was interviewing Hinton, not Tiant, but it didn't matter because he couldn't understand half of what Hinton was saying anyway."

• • • • •

"One time we were going on a road trip in spring training and, in those days, everybody had to carry his own equipment bag. Gary Bell, who was one of the all-time funniest guys I ever knew, put two dead jackrabbits in Tiant's bag. You can imagine what happened when Looie opened his bag. The dead jackrabbits scared the hell out of him. Nobody ever told him it was Bell who did it, but I think Looie knew, because Bell was always doing things like that."

• • • • •

"After Albert Belle left and returned [to Jacobs Field] as a visiting player, he always was pretty nice, except one night [1999] when he was playing for Baltimore. He was mad because he was having a bad game. After every time he batted and didn't get a hit, he came into the clubhouse, took a cup of All-Sport [drink], sipped from it, and then threw the rest on the floor, all over the carpet.

"I don't know if he was trying to get on me or what, but I just let it go. I'd wipe it up and not say anything. When the season ended, the [Indians] ball club sent him a bill for cleaning the carpet. I don't know how much they charged him, but it was a lot. Probably about $500. I didn't know what to expect from him the following season. He never said anything to me about it, but he didn't spill any more All-Sport on the carpet."

• • • • •

"When Belle first came up with us, after he made an out he'd take a bat—anybody's bat that was laying around—and swing it against the wall and break it. I told him, 'Albert, I don't mind if you break a bat, but one of these times you're going to hurt your hand and it'll be goodbye to your career.'

"After that he took my advice about not hitting the wall but instead, went down where the john was located and started hitting the door on the partition.

"He did it so many times he broke the partition, not the bat he was swinging, and when the season ended Art Modell's company [that owned the Stadium] sent him a bill for repairing the john. That one cost him about $2,500, which he couldn't believe. As far as I know, he paid it."

Rocky Colavito
(Outfielder, 1955-1959, 1965-1967)

Just as thousands of Indians fans never forgave Frank Lane for trading Rocky Colavito to the Detroit Tigers [for Harvey Kuenn] in 1960, neither has the principal.

"Let me put it this way," Colavito said during a 2002 visit to Cleveland, "I never thought [Lane] was a good person, OK? And when you're not a good person when you're alive, you're not a good person when you're dead. By that I mean, when somebody dies a lot of people want to make that person out to have been an angel, but I don't believe in that baloney. That's a lot of ... well, you know. It's a farce.

"And [Lane] was not a good person. I never thought he was a good human being, and that was very important to me. I also thought he was a terrible baseball man. He couldn't see; he had such bad eyesight, so how could he tell a good ballplayer?

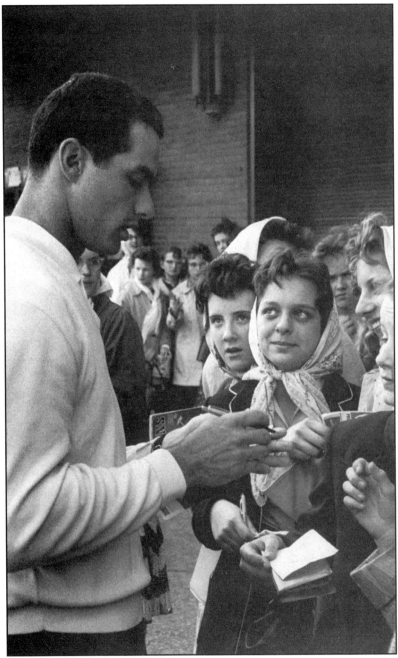

Rocky Colavito signs autographs for his adoring fans in Cleveland.
George Silk/Time Life Pictures/Getty Images

"He also was an egomaniac. He had his secretary go through 35 newspapers a day to find references to his name. He knew if he made a deal of any magnitude, it would get his name on the front page. We should've won the pennant [in 1960], but he decimated the entire team with his crazy deals."

• • • • •

It was during that visit to Cleveland that, among the fans asking Colavito for his autograph, was a boy who called the former outfielder his "all-time favorite" player.

"I asked him, 'How can I be your favorite player when you weren't even born when I played here?' He said, 'Because my mother always talked about how good you were.'

"And if that doesn't warm your heart, as it did mine, nothing will."

Vince Colbert
(Pitcher, 1970-1972)

"When I came up with the Indians, they had a relief pitcher named Fred Lasher, and he and [manager] Alvin Dark never seemed to see eye to eye about things, especially about how Lasher was being used," recalled Vince Colbert, also a relief pitcher.

"One night when Fred was pitching, Alvin walked out to the mound, stuck his hand out, and said, 'Fred, give me the ball.' But instead of handing the ball to Dark, Lasher slammed it to the ground and stalked off the mound. As Fred was walking to the dugout, the fans behind the dugout started booing him, and Fred got so pissed off, he threw his glove at the fans.

"Well, back then, those things weren't collector's items like they are now, and the fan who caught the glove threw it back at Fred. It was one of the funniest things I ever saw.

"After that, Fred didn't last long. Alvin told him to get out of here, and he was gone … never came back," Colbert said, though Lasher pitched briefly, appearing in two games for the California Angels in 1971 and then was out of baseball.

• • • • •

"I got along OK with Dark, but when Ken Aspromonte took over as manager [in 1972], he and [then-president–general manager] Gabe Paul thought I would be more effective if I lost some weight. A lot of weight.

"I remember it as clearly as if it happened yesterday. Aspromonte called me in mid-January [1972] and said they wanted me to come to camp at 190 pounds. *One hundred-and-ninety pounds!* Geez, I hadn't been that light since I couldn't remember when. At the time I was pitching anywhere from 215 to 220.

"But in those days you did as you were told, and I went on a crash diet and lost more than 30 pounds. All I'd do, basically, was have a cup of black coffee and a piece of toast when I got up in the morning. For lunch I'd have another cup of black coffee and maybe a piece of fruit. Something like that. That was it. I was determined to get down to what they wanted. I finally did. I got down to 190.

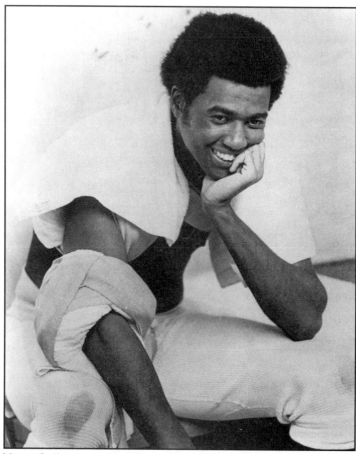

Vince Colbert ices his elbow after pitching. Colbert was asked to lose weight by the Indians staff, but once he did, he lost power and speed in his pitching. Russell Schneider Collection

"The trouble was, in addition to losing all that weight, I also lost a lot of strength—and the steam on my fastball. I couldn't throw hard at all. Until then my fastball ranged in the low 90s. But not after I got down to 190. It was awful. People who knew me asked if I had been sick because I was so thin, so gaunt looking. In fact, when I got to spring training, they ran tests on me because they thought I might have sickle cell anemia or something.

"I didn't realize at the time what I did to myself, going on that crash diet, but it wound up costing me my career. It took me more than two years to regain my weight and my strength, but by then it was too late. The Indians just gave up on me. They told me I didn't have it anymore. And it didn't help to gain back the weight because, to do so, I ate the wrong things. I got my weight back, but not my strength.

"As I said, things were different then. A lot different.

"I like to believe that if the Indians had left me alone, if they had not told me to lose weight—for my own good, they said—everything would have turned out differently, and I would have had a better career, certainly a longer career. But that's my only real regret."

Del Crandall
(Catcher, 1966)

Prior to joining the Indians, Del Crandall played 15 seasons in the National League for the Boston/Milwaukee Braves, San Francisco Giants, and Pittsburgh Pirates, during which he caught Hall of Fame pitchers Warren Spahn and Juan Marichal, as well as Lew Burdette and Bob Veale.

It gave him unique insight in comparing them with Sam McDowell, who in 1970 was at the peak of what should also have been a Hall of Fame career.

"Sam McDowell's fastball, slider, curve, and change-up—all four of his pitches—were as good as any guy I ever caught."

Coco Crisp
(Outfielder, 2002-)

It would seem that Coco Crisp has an easy time of it, signing autographs, because his name contains only nine letters—four in his nickname and five in his surname. But that's not necessarily so, he said. "It's no big deal, but when someone asks for my autograph, I usually sign my full name," which is *Cavelli* Crisp.

He was nicknamed Coco by his grandmother when he was an infant.

"A lot of people ask me why I always look so serious, but I'm not really a serious guy," he said. "I clown around a lot, except when I step on the field, and especially not when I'm up to bat. Then I'm very serious. I know baseball is a game, but it's my job, and I know I have to focus when I'm on the field. I'll clown around in the clubhouse and off the field, but not on the field."

• • • • •

When he dropped a routine fly ball for an error in the Tribe's 2004 season opener against Minnesota, Crisp explained, "It was textbook. I saw the ball all the way as it was coming down. I held up my glove. The ball is supposed to go into my glove. I close my glove, and the ball stays there. But that time, I did my job. The ball didn't do its job."

• • • • •

Another time later that season, in a game against the New York Yankees, Crisp slapped a grounder down the first-base line that pitcher Orlando Hernandez fielded. Instead of tossing the ball to the first baseman, Hernandez straddled the line and waited with his arms folded to tag Crisp.

But Coco had other ideas. He faked a move to the left and then another to the right, but still Hernandez didn't bite, just held his ground, waiting for Crisp.

Finally the umpire called Coco out for leaving the baseline.

"I tried to juke him, but he wouldn't fall for it," said Crisp—who enjoyed the failed maneuver as much as the fans did.

Jeff Datz
(Coach, 2002-)

"One night during a game [then-manager] Charlie Manuel made a call that something was going to happen, and it was one of the damndest things I ever saw," Jeff Datz recalled from the 2002 season.

"Jim Thome was batting, and when the other team's pitching coach—I don't want to say who it was—started to the mound, Charlie tapped me on the shoulder and said, 'Watch this, Big Daddy,' which is what he sometimes called me, 'Jimmy is good for a home run, right now.'

"When the coach finished talking to his pitcher, he walked back to the dugout and Charlie tapped me on the arm again. 'I'm telling you, Big Daddy,' he said, 'watch this. After that conversation we're good for a home run. Jimmy is going deep right here.' And damned if it didn't happen just like that. Thome hit the first pitch into the right-field seats. Wow! I couldn't believe it."

•   •   •   •   •

After pitching batting practice before a game during a hot spell in July 2004, Datz remarked, "It's so hot out there I saw a dog chasing a cat and they were both walking."

Jason Davis
(Pitcher, 2002-)

After getting his first look at the Big Apple during the Indians' first series in New York in 2003, Jason Davis, who was born and raised in Chattanooga, Tennessee, said, "I bet there are more people in this town than there are in all of Tennessee."

(For the record, the population of Tennessee in 2002 was 5,797,289 people; New York City recorded 8,008,278 residents in 2002.)

Larry Doby
(Outfielder, 1947-1955, 1958)

Before he died in 2003, Larry Doby talked about how he had wanted to coach and manage in the major leagues after he retired as a player with the Chicago White Sox and Montreal, in addition to the Indians, but that he knew because of the way baseball had changed that the game had "passed me by."

"The discipline that was in place when I played doesn't seem to be there anymore. I couldn't see myself

Larry Doby takes a break on the trainer's table. Francis Miller/Time Life Pictures/Getty Images

saying to a player, 'I am going to sit you down and fine you, blah, blah, blah,' and then have him go upstairs and complain to the front office or for the players union to tell me I couldn't do this or that, even though I was the manager of the team.

"Because of the money the players are making today, and the rules that are in effect, you can't fine a guy enough to make it meaningful, which is a shame."

Frank Duffy
(Shortstop, 1972-1977)

Though his highest batting average was only .263 (in 1973) and his 10-year major league record was only .232, Frank Duffy was considered one of baseball's best short-stops and probably could have extended his career instead of retiring in 1979 after he'd been traded to Boston the previous season. But he had no regrets about leaving the game at the age of 32.

"When I retired I actually had a feeling of relief," he said. "I knew it was time for me to go. I had other objectives. I wanted to find out what it was like to live in the real world. I was tired of the whole routine [of Major League Baseball], the regimentation.

"It got to be like the military—you have to be on the bus at a certain time, at the airport at a certain time, at the ballpark at a certain time—it was more than I wanted to live with. I still wake up some mornings and think how glad I am that I don't have to catch a bus, or be at an airport, or get to the game.

"Sure, baseball was good to me. I made some money that helped me get started in the real estate business, and I'm grateful for what baseball did for me. But that part of my life is behind me. I'm facing new challenges now."

Dave Duncan
(Catcher, 1973-1974)

Since leaving the Indians, Dave Duncan has become one of baseball's most highly respected pitching coaches (under manager Tony La Russa with Oakland from 1986 to 1995 and St. Louis from 1996 to the present).

He also played for the Kansas City/Oakland Athletics (1964-1972) and Baltimore (1975-1976), and despite his brief tenure with the Indians, Duncan has the highest regard for Cleveland and its fans.

"Cleveland is the only place I played where you can drive 100 miles away from the city, walk into a store, and have somebody ask you about the team. The fans in Cleveland are tremendous."

Steve Dunning
(Pitcher, 1970-1973)

"It was overwhelming to be drafted No. 1 in the country [in 1970] and then to be given the opportunity to pitch in the big leagues immediately—and to win," said Steve Dunning, who started and hurled five innings in a 9-2 victory over the Milwaukee Brewers on June 14, 1970.

"It was almost beyond comprehension—a dream come true, something I'll never forget as long as I live. And if I could play my [seven-year major league] career over again, the only part I'd change would be the middle and end, certainly not the beginning."

After beating the Brewers in his first professional baseball game fresh out of Stanford University, Dunning said, "I'm so excited and jubilant and happy. This is the greatest thrill of my life. It is a magnificent moment, a fairy tale. I'm not even sure it is real."

Dennis Eckersley
(Pitcher, 1975-1977)

"I can still pitch, I just can't get anybody out," quipped Dennis Eckersley upon his annual return to Cleveland in 2003 for a fundraiser on behalf of his late agent, Ed Keating.

Eckersley sure could pitch—and get batters out—when he broke in as a starter with the Indians in 1975 and pitched a no-hitter against the California Angels on May 30, 1977. He was traded to Boston in 1978, then to the Chicago Cubs in 1984, and in 1987 to Oakland where he launched his Hall of Fame career as one of the greatest relief pitchers in baseball history under manager Tony La Russa. He pitched for St. Louis in 1996-1997 and ended his outstanding career back in Boston in 1998.

Eckersley, with a 197-171 won-lost record and 390 saves in 1,071 games, was inducted into the Hall of Fame in 2004, in his first year of eligibility.

Eckersley's reformation as a pitcher—from starter to ace reliever—virtually coincided with his reformation as an alcoholic.

"I am an alcoholic and was out of control," he said. "It began when I was in Cleveland and continued until I hit bottom in January 1987, when I finally went into rehab, which saved my life. If I hadn't gotten a second chance, I probably would have wound up the same as my brother Wallace. He's in prison serving a 40-year sentence for attempted kidnapping and attempted murder. That's what drugs and alcohol did to him."

It's the reason Eckersley returns to Cleveland every year to raise money for Keating's project, the Freedom House, a rehab center for young men trying to break loose from drug and alcohol addiction.

"I enjoyed my time with the Indians. I didn't want to leave. When I was traded [to Boston] I cried like a baby. I loved being a member of the Indians. But I guess it was only natural for me to feel that way. The first time you get traded is huge, because you are so close to so many players. I was close to Buddy Bell and quite a few guys. I didn't want to go. It's like college or something. You build such closeness to your teammates. It doesn't matter if you're on a .500 team, you want to stay right there.

"Little did I know that there were a lot of great things ahead for me."

Ed Farmer
(Pitcher, 1971-1973)

When he first came up with the Indians as a 21-year-old pitcher, Ed Farmer admitted, "I was kind of embarrassed because my father had filled out my [publicity] bio for me. In it he wrote that I had said my goal was to win both the Cy Young Award and the Most Valuable Player award in the same year—in my first year in the big leagues.

"He meant well and did it to motivate me, but you can imagine what the veterans on the team thought when they read what I was supposed to have said. And then when one of the writers read it and wrote it in the paper, it got picked up by other papers around the league, and I really got kidded a lot. Chuck Hinton was on my back about it for a long time."

• • • • •

After Farmer was traded by the Indians on June 17, 1973, he went on to pitch for Detroit, Philadelphia, Baltimore, Milwaukee, Texas, Chicago White Sox, and Philadelphia again and Oakland through 1983 and for the last several years has been a broadcaster for the White Sox.

"I went to arbitration in the winter of 1980-1981 after I appeared in 64 games for the White Sox, had a 7-9 record with a 3.34 earned run average, and saved 30 games, which was then a club record. I did all that with a team that won only 70 games all season. Not only did I save 30, I pitched 99 innings, and, nowadays if you are a short man and you pitch maybe 40 or 42 innings or something like that, you're doing good.

"My 30 saves were second most in the American League to Goose Gossage and Dan Quisenberry, who each had 33, but their teams [the New York Yankees and Kansas City Royals] both won the ALCS for the pennant. I asked for a $495,000 salary, which was $365,000 more than I made in 1980, and $145,000 more than the White Sox were offering.

"The arbitrator was a man named Theodore J. St. Antoine, who was the chairman of the law school at the University of Michigan. He listened to the presentations by my agent, Steve Greenberg, and by the ball club, which took about two and a half hours. The arbitrator compared my record to the other guys' numbers, which is the way those things go, and finally the hearing ended and he said he would consider the arguments and make a decision in a few days.

"But then, as my agent and I got up and walked to the door to leave the room, we were called back by St. Antoine. He said, 'I have a question. I'm just not clear on one thing.' My agent said, 'OK, what is it?' And he said, 'Tell me … what is a save?' We couldn't believe our ears.

"I told him, 'Well, it's like when a war is going on and the enemy is closing in to capture the city, and I'm the only guy out there and keep them from capturing the city. That's a save.'

"He said, 'Oh, and that's it? That's a save? And you had 30 of them?' I said, 'Yes, that's it. So help me.' That's the way it went.

"A couple days later I was getting ready to fly with my family from California to Florida, and I called my agent. He wasn't in, and his secretary said she wasn't supposed to tell me if we won or lost. I told her, 'All I want to know is if this is going to be a happy flight or a sad flight.'

"She said, 'Well, let me tell you this. We have champagne here in the office, and it's open.' That's how I found out that we won.

"Here's a sidebar to that story. After I won the arbitration case, I got paid over 12 months, instead of six, as had been the case previously, and when I got my first big pay-check—it was for $39,000 after taxes and other stuff—I showed it to my wife, Barbara. She said, 'I thought you were making a half million dollars. That check doesn't look like much more than you brought home last year.'

"I said, 'No, Barbara. Look again. Now the comma is *behind* the nine, not in front of it, as it was the year before when I was getting, like, $3,900 every two weeks, after deductions."

• • • • •

In 1991, eight years after his pitching career ended, Farmer was diagnosed with terminal kidney disease. He underwent a successful kidney transplantation—Farmer's donor was his younger brother Tom—and since then has been active in the Kidney Foundation.

Because of his celebrity status as one of baseball's premier relief pitchers and now as a major league broadcaster and Kidney Foundation spokesman, Farmer said he often uses an alias when he registers in a hotel on the road.

Among the names he said he used were, "Chuck Roast, Dakota Smith, and Cheyenne Bailey, although I have others that I'll keep to myself."

Bob Feller
(Pitcher, 1936-1941, 1945-1956)

Bob Feller's autograph is one of the most sought after and one of the easiest to get because he makes himself readily available to fans everywhere, which led to the following quip: "A guy came up to me and wanted me to sign a picture. I told him, 'I thought everybody in the United States already had my autograph or didn't want it.'"

• • • • •

The outspoken Hall of Fame pitcher often is asked about one of his few disappointments in baseball—that he never won a World Series game.

"In 1954, after we lost the first three games, Al Lopez came back with Bob Lemon instead of starting me. I guess he thought Lemon had a better chance to win the fourth game because he'd had a great year, won over 20 games [23]. He pitched real well in the opener even though we lost 5-2 on a 10th-inning bloop home run by Dusty Rhodes that only went about 250 feet, maybe 251, down the right-field foul line. Rhodes hit the ball on the handle of his bat and [right fielder] Dave Pope almost caught it.

"I was just spot starting that particular year. I wasn't throwing as hard in 1954 as I did in my prime, even though I still won 13 games mainly with curves and sliders—and with smoke and mirrors. Leo Durocher said to me later that he'd told his ball club that I was the only pitcher they might not be able to beat, and several players confirmed it to me. But the Giants were hot. [Johnny] Antonelli pitched well, they got some very timely hitting, and Durocher did a good job of managing.

"Lopez never talked to me about not starting a game in the Series, and I never asked him about it, so I have no idea what his strategy was or why he didn't let me pitch. But Lemon never could pitch with only two days' rest. Everybody in the league knew it and Bob knew it himself.

Al probably thought, well, maybe our luck would change [in the fourth game].

"I don't bear any resentment toward Lopez. I just think it was bad strategy. There was nothing personal about it. I don't care if he had pitched me or not, but he never should have pitched Lemon in my opinion.

"As for my losing [1-0] the opening game of the 1948 World Series [against the then-Boston Braves], when people ask me about the pickoff play that was screwed up by National League umpire Bill Stewart in the eighth inning, I remind them that it cost me a tie game, not a victory.

"The Braves won because I made the mistake of walking the leadoff batter, Bill Salkeld. And it was Phil Masi [Salkeld's pinch runner] who was called safe on the pickoff play, which enabled him to score the only run [on a single by Tommy Holmes].

"When you walk the leadoff batter in an inning, he's going to score 80 or 90 percent of the time. That was the mistake that hurt me as much—maybe more—than the mistake the umpire made, which everybody knew was a mistake.

"Boudreau had planned to tell the umpires and alert them to our pickoff play so they wouldn't also get picked off. But when Boudreau met with them in the commissioner's meeting the day before the Series began, he didn't say anything because [Boston Braves manager] Billy Southworth was there and he didn't want to alert him as well as the umpires.

"We won the Series, which was more important than the disappointment I felt [in losing Game 1 and and also Game 5 11-5]."

• • • • •

"One winter when I was nine or 10 years old, I went to see Lou Gehrig and Babe Ruth play an exhibition game on their barnstorming tour. Their teams were named the 'Larrupin' Lous' and 'Bustin' Babes,' and I got both of them to autograph a ball that I'd bought for five dollars. I raised the money to buy the ball by catching 50 gophers, which were overrunning the farms in the area.

"Those gophers would burrow into the ground and ruin the crops, so the county put out a bounty of 10 cents for each pair of claws we turned in. We'd catch them and kill them by putting them in a bag connected to the exhaust system of our old Dodge truck, then cut their claws off, and take them to the treasurer's office and collect our money.

"Ruth retired [from the Boston Bees] in 1935, one year before I got to the big leagues with the Indians. But I did get to pitch against Gehrig for two and a half seasons. Lou was a big, strong guy, and even though he was not a real good curveball hitter, he could hit a fastball a mile. Especially if you got the ball up.

"I used to throw him a lot of overhand curve balls and kind of wasted my fastball. And, when I did throw him a fastball, I tried to keep it down and in. He was so strong; he had a lot of power and could hit the ball out of any park, in any direction, even though he was basically a pull hitter. He also was a very good first baseman, a very quiet fellow who smoked quite a bit.

"The Babe was different. He was kind of a blunt guy who smoked big cigars and was known to take a drink now

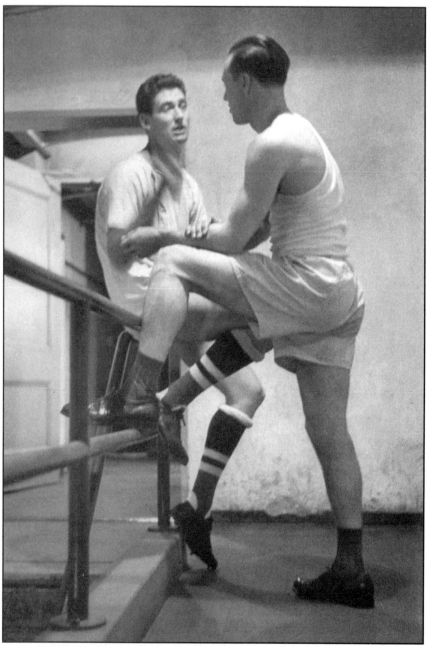

Bob Feller (foreground) got to pitch against and watch some of the greatest baseball players of the game, including Ted Williams. Hy Peskin/Time Life Pictures/Getty Images

and then—even more than now and then—which Gehrig did not.

• • • • •

When someone called Feller a "hero" because he enlisted in the navy two days after the start of World War II and then spent 44 months aboard the battleship USS *Alabama* during the prime of his career, he said: "I wasn't a hero. I was a survivor. The heroes didn't come back. The survivors returned."

And, as for his 266 victories in his 18-year major league career, Feller said, "There's only one win that was worth it to me … and that was World War II."

• • • • •

In the press box one night a visiting scribe asked Feller about the then-ongoing scandal involving players' uses of steroids and growth hormones.

"Did the players in your day take anything to make themselves bigger, stronger, faster?" the reporter wanted to know.

Feller's deadpan response: "Yes—it was called Wheaties."

Ray Fosse
(Catcher, 1967-1972, 1976-1977)

"Sam McDowell and I were on the American League All-Star team in 1970, and the night before the game the two of us and our wives were having dinner in the hotel dining room," said Ray Fosse as he recalled one of the most significant incidents of his 12-year major league career.

"Pete Rose came into the hotel dining room and asked Sam and me if we were doing anything special. We weren't, so he invited us—Sam and his wife and me and my wife—over to his house.

"Later, about midnight or 1 a.m.—it was no later than 1 a.m.—Pete took us back to the hotel. We had a nice time. There was no drinking, nothing like that; it was just a nice visit.

"But a funny thing happened—though, in retrospect, it really wasn't so funny. Pete's story changed over the years, which is amazing, maybe because Pete has amnesia or something. What bothers me and has for a long time is that the man keeps telling a different story. If he would just tell the truth about everything, I'd feel a lot different.

"He doesn't mention that we were all together and that we were back at 1 a.m., not 4 a.m. as he has told the story; he also fails to say that we weren't drinking, and that Sam and I were not alone, that we had our wives with us, which he has never said. Those are the things that bother me."

It was in the 12th inning of the 1970 All-Star Game the next day that Pete crashed into Fosse, scoring the National League's winning run for a 5-4 victory and causing an injury to the catcher that hampered him the rest of his career.

"When the play [the collision with Rose] began, Pete was on second base and the batter was Jim Hickman, who hit the pitch to center field. Amos Otis [the AL center fielder] charged the ball and, as Pete was coming around third, I positioned myself to where I thought Otis's throw would come, which happened to be up the line.

"If I had stayed on home plate, I would have missed the ball by three or four feet. I was looking straight out to center field and all of a sudden [Rose] hit me. I never saw him coming. It was total shock. I wasn't braced. All I wanted to do was catch the ball, and he smoked me.

"I knew I was hurt because I couldn't move my left shoulder. But I told everybody it was OK.

"Our first game after the All-Star Game was in Kansas City, it was a doubleheader, and when I caught the first game, Sam was on the mound throwing 100 miles an hour. I couldn't lift my left arm above my shoulder; it was so sore, but I went on playing through the end of the season. It wasn't until the following April that I realized I had fractured and separated my left shoulder.

"Remember, that was [34 years] ago, and things were different then. I was making 12 grand, and in those days, if a bone wasn't sticking out of your body they'd say, 'You're OK … go ahead and play.'

"It's different now. Players are really protected. But then, hey, in our day, you played. Period. Pete says he missed two or three games afterward because of the collision, but it was his thigh that was bruised. That's all.

"Sure, it hurt my career. Definitely. I had 16 home runs at the time of the All-Star Game, and when I took batting practice in Kansas City the first day we were back, I could hardly swing the bat. Everything was a swing with my right arm. Every time I think about it, I wonder, could I have been a 30-home run hitter? And could I continue to hit 30 to 35 home runs a year?

"Yeah, I think I could have—but I didn't. I still think, if things back then were the way they are now, the way they take care of guys, it all might have been different for me."

· · · · ·

On catching Sam McDowell, Fosse said, "Sam had four of the greatest pitches of any pitcher I ever caught. I mean, he had a helluva fastball, hard-breaking curve, quick slider, and a real good change-up, and he was consistent with all of them.

"Sam was funny about some things, one of them was that he wanted to call his own pitches, so we let him most of the time. He'd do it by adding or subtracting from the numbers I'd put down, by brushing up or down with his glove against his uniform shirt.

"But sometimes it would get to be a problem, especially when I first started catching Sam. I'd signal for a pitch—we usually used two and five [fingers] for a fastball, one for a curve, three for a slider, and four for a change-up. Then Sam could add or subtract from my numbers to change the call.

"Here's how we did it. Say, I'd put down two fingers for a fastball, and he'd add three by brushing his glove three times, which would be his signal for a fastball, same as mine when I put two fingers down. I'd look out at him and wonder, 'What are you doing?' I had just called for a fastball. Basically, I think he just wanted everyone to know that he was calling his own game.

"Everybody talked about how hard he threw, which he did, but he also had a great change-up and loved to fool batters with it. He liked to do it so much that sometimes he'd throw the change-up without even telling me. I'd be looking for a fastball and he'd change up on me.

"Now, as a catcher, I don't care if you throw a change-up off a fastball signal. But when there was a runner on first base, I had to be ready in case he tried to steal, and I didn't want to be looking fastball and have the hitter hit me in the back of the head with his bat because Sam threw a change-up. When he'd do that, when Sam would throw me a change-up when I was looking for a fastball, I'd tell him, 'Hey, I'm on your side, don't try to fool me.'

"After we were together a few years, I figured out that he was tipping off his pitches—every time he was going to throw a fastball he'd take his glove over his head, and when he'd throw a change-up, his glove would go straight up. Because I learned to recognize what was coming, I'd catch his change-up without any trouble, and he'd look at me like, 'How'd you catch that?' He was really a piece of work."

• • • • •

After his retirement as a player in 1979, Fosse returned to Cleveland often as a broadcaster for the Oakland Athletics. And although he hadn't played for the Indians since 1977, there was one occasion in 2004 when he was walking in the downtown area and was surprised to be recognized and greeted by an old fan.

"He was a cop and said to me, 'Hey, you're Ray Fosse, aren't you?' I told him I was and he said, 'I watched you play for the Indians,' and I said, 'You must have been two or three years old.'"

Julio Franco
(Shortstop and second baseman,
1983-1988, 1996-1997)

"I'm ageless," said Julio Franco, who initially came to the Indians as a rookie shortstop in a trade with Philadelphia in 1983.

Since an aborted comeback with the Tribe in 1997 he has played baseball all over the world, including Japan in 1998, Mexico in 1999, Korea in 2000, and Mexico again in 2001.

Franco signed with Atlanta at the tail end of 2001 and has been a key member of the Braves the last three seasons, extending his major league service to nine teams—Texas, the Chicago White Sox, Milwaukee, and Tampa Bay, in addition to the Phillies, Indians, and Braves—in a professional career that now spans 27 years and counting.

As he said during the 2004 season, "I want to play five more years. Why not? Age doesn't mean you're old. Your body will tell you when you're old. My body tells me, 'Julio, you were born to play baseball, so keep playing.' God gave me the gift to play for a long time, and I am honoring Him. If you can keep playing, why not? If you are 21 and hit a double or if you're 40 and hit a double, it's still a double."

As for Franco's official chronological age, the Indians' and Braves' media guides, as well as *The Baseball Encyclopedia*, say he was born August 23, 1958, which would have made him 46 in 2004.

Franco evaded a direct answer when pointedly asked how old he was in the winter of 2003-2004.

"I'm 51, no, 43 ... and [the Braves] say, 45. When they took our pictures, they asked us questions [for the media guide] and one of them was, 'Can you tell us something about you that nobody else knows?'

"I wrote down, 'My age,'" Franco told the Braves and left it at that. So be it.

Richie Garcia
(Supervisor of umpires)

"In 1974, my first season as an American League umpire, I had a little problem with the Indians and even bigger problems with them in 1976," recalled Richie Garcia, who had a reputation for being strong willed— OK, *hot-headed*—before he was promoted to a supervisory position in 2003.

"I think I had 14 ejections in 1976, and out of those 14, a lot of them were Indians players. I had a little bit of a feud going with Rocky Colavito [then the Tribe's first base coach under manager Frank Robinson], and I ran him a couple of times, once because he bumped me—or I bumped him, whatever.

"Anyway, Rocky and I had a mutual friend, Frank Cozza, who lived in Anaheim and owned a restaurant. I was in town and so were the Indians, and my friend Cozza called me and said, 'C'mon over after the game and I'll fix something for you and some of the guys to eat.' So I did. No problem. I had [fellow umpire] Ron Luciano with me, and we went to Frank's house.

"But unbeknownst to me, he also invited Rocky, Herb Score [then a Tribe broadcaster], and a couple of Indians players.

"So we went to Cozza's place, and he's got this big table set up with food, and I walk in the room and there's Rocky Colavito. I'm like, oh, my God!

"But you know what? It probably was the best thing that could have happened because Rocky and I talked about the things that had happened between us, why they happened, how they happened, and we patched things up. Our feud was over, and we became good friends, which was the reason Frank Cozza set it all up. Frank was a good friend to both Rocky and me—and still is."

Wayne Garland
(Pitcher, 1977-1981)

"It was a long time ago and only God knows what might have happened—or wouldn't have happened—if I had not signed that big contract with the Indians," said Wayne Garland, who was one of baseball's first free agents back in 1977.

Garland was coming off a 20-7 and 2.67 ERA season with the Baltimore Orioles and was offered a 10-year $2.3 million contract by Ted Bonda, then principal owner of the Indians, and his general manager, Phil Seghi.

"If I'd turned down Cleveland's offer and stayed with the Orioles, maybe I wouldn't have hurt my shoulder," said Garland who suffered a torn rotator cuff in 1978 and underwent surgery the following year but was never the same. "I'm sure the pressure to excel beyond my capabilities was a factor in what happened to me. I wanted to prove that I was worth the money the Indians were paying me.

"But then, nobody but God really knows."

One thing Garland does know: "I didn't ask for what the Indians gave me, and I would have been a fool to turn it down."

Ironically, his contract averaged only $230,000 a season—and in 2003 the major league *minimum* salary was $230,000 for one season.

"Now, the 25th player on a roster makes as much as I did as the so-called '2.3 million dollar man,' as [the media] called me in 1977."

In his nine seasons as a major league pitcher, Garland won 55 games and lost 66 (his five-year record with the Indians was 28-48) before quitting the game at the end of 1981, although he coached at the minor league level for a few years after hanging up his glove.

Jody Gerut
(Outfielder, 2003-)

After playing right field against New York for the first time in Yankee Stadium, Jody Gerut said, "It's like a college crowd. They have an ugly chant that ends with 'Jody, you're ugly.' I also heard a lot of 'mother' comments, too."

Jim "Mudcat" Grant
(Pitcher, 1958-1964)

Upon reading during the winter of 2003-2004 that two National Hockey League teams had declared bankruptcy, "Mudcat" Grant said, "That reminds me of how poor the Indians were back in my days with the team.

"Nobody ever admitted it publicly, but I know the reason the Indians traded me to Minnesota in 1964 was because they couldn't afford my salary. It wasn't that I was making so much money, it was simply because the Indians didn't have it. They were cutting payroll every chance they got but always lied about it, saying they were trading this player or that player because the one they were getting was the guy they really wanted.

"Yeah, sure. And who was the guy they got for me? Jack Kralick, which should tell you something."

Kralick's five-year won-lost record with Cleveland was 33-33, and in his nine-year major league career it was 67-65. Grant was 50-35 with the Twins from 1964 to 1967, became the first black starting pitcher to win 20 decisions and a World Series game in 1965 and ended his 14-year major league career in 1971 with a 145-119 overall won-lost record.

•   •   •   •   •

"One of the funniest things I remember about my pitching career in Cleveland," Grant said, "involved catcher Joe Azcue and umpire Ed Hurley in 1964.

"We were having a lot of trouble with Hurley that year, so before the second game of a doubleheader that I was going to pitch, I went outside the Stadium where the mounted policemen were stationed. I scooped up some fresh horse manure, put it in a can, and took it into the clubhouse.

"Then I smeared [the manure] all over the [back] straps of Azcue's chest protector so that Hurley [umpiring behind the plate] would get a good whiff of it every time he bent over Joe to call a pitch.

"Well, as the game went on, I could tell that Hurley noticed it, and although he never said anything, every inning he'd back up farther behind Azcue.

"Finally, about the fourth or fifth inning Hurley called [manager] Birdie Tebbetts on the field and told him, 'Birdie, you better get your catcher out of here—he really needs a shower.'

"Well, Azcue stayed in the game, but because he smelled so bad—or at least because Hurley thought it was Joe who smelled so bad—we got out of there in a hurry. I think the game was over in less than two hours."

•   •   •   •   •

"My mother was the greatest influence on my life, my greatest inspiration. Once, when I was growing up in Lacoochee, [Florida], she sat me down with a glass of water in front of me and put a cork in the glass. Then she put her finger on the cork and held it down under the water until she took her hand away and the cork would come back up to the top of the water.

"She told me, 'You be like this cork. Every time you get down, you can always bounce back if you keep on trying. Keep on working. Don't give up. Never give up.'"

Steve Gromek
(Pitcher, 1941-1953)

"A game I remember so well, one of my favorites, although the result wasn't as good, was the first one I pitched in the big leagues," Steve Gromek remembered. "The Indians brought me up from Flint [of the Class C Michigan State League] when I was only 21 years old. I went out to the mound for my first game, and I was shaking like a leaf. Rollie Hemsley was supposed to catch me, but he told [manager] Roger Peckinpaugh, 'I'm not going to catch that kid. ... He's too wild. He's going to be all over the place.'

"So Peckinpaugh put in Gene Desautels, and after I pitched good, even though I lost to Washington 4-2, Hemsley came over and apologized. He told me he'd said what he did to Peckinpaugh for my benefit, to motivate me—but I'm not sure he was right about that."

Ricky Gutierrez
(Second baseman, 2002-2003)

Ricky Gutierrez didn't play much for the Indians, due to injuries, and spent almost as much time in extended spring training in Winter Haven, Florida, as he did in Cleveland. It motivated him to declare, "Some days it was so hot down there I swear I saw the devil come up and stand beside me."

Travis Hafner
(First baseman and designated hitter, 2003-)

Travis Hafner was holding a base runner, Armando Rios, on first base with Danys Baez on the mound against Chicago and with Joe Crede at bat during a game on June 1, 2003. Crede hit a liner that Baez caught while lunging in the direction of first base.

Although Rios was only about two or three steps off the base, Baez, in full adrenaline rush—and only about 20 feet from Hafner—wound up and fired a fastball to the first baseman, attempting to double Rios off the base.

"When I saw him wind up I thought to myself, 'Oh, no!' Hafner said. "Luckily, the ball hit me in the chest, not in the face or somewhere else that it could have really hurt and rolled down into my glove. After the game Omar [Vizquel] suggested that I play first base wearing a [catcher's] mask."

• • • • •

After he hit for the cycle against Minnesota on August 14, 2003, becoming the first member of an Indians team in 25 years to hit a homer, triple, double, and single in the same game, Hafner said, "I'm trying to think of something clever to say."

Then, when kidded about how he lumbered around the bases on his triple, Hafner said, "I felt like I was flying, until I saw the replay on TV. Geez, I might be the slowest person in baseball."

• • • • •

How did Hafner come to be nicknamed "Pronk"?

"It started in spring training my first year with the Indians. It's supposed to mean I'm part project and part donkey because, first, Bill Selby called me 'The Project,' then other guys started calling me 'Big Donkey.'

"So, one day Selby put the two together. 'Pronk.' That simple."

When someone suggested that he drop the project part of his nickname, considering the fact that, at the time during the 2004 season Hafner was batting .324 with 21 homers, he thought for a minute and said, 'But then I'd just be Donk. No, 'Pronk' is good enough."

• • • • •

"My high school [in Jamestown, North Dakota] was so small we didn't have a baseball team, so in the spring I competed in track, even though I was bad in everything. At track meets the top six finishers would place [earn points], but sometimes there weren't even six in an event, and if there were less than six, I'd enter. I'd go from event to event seeing if they had enough people entered. If they didn't, I'd enter. I'd run the two mile, the 110 hurdles, triple jump—anything to try to get some points for my school."

When his high school counselor asked Hafner—who was one of only eight students in his senior class—what his career aspiration was upon graduation, Hafner said he wanted to be a professional baseball player.

Travis Hafner's batting has been a valuable asset to the Indians.
David Maxwell/Getty Images

"When the counselor asked if I had a No. 2 choice, I said baseball was my No. 1 choice and my No. 2 choice. He didn't ask if I had a third choice, but it would have been the same."

• • • • •

When he was on the online fan ballot for the 2004 American League All-Star team (along with Lew Ford of the Minnesota Twins, Hideki Matsui of the New York Yankees, and Frank Thomas and Paul Konerko of the Chicago White Sox) to be chosen for the 32nd and final place on the team, Hafner politicked for votes.

"I brought my laptop computer to the clubhouse so my teammates could vote for me," and said his slogan was, "Vote Pronk."

It helped, but not enough. Matsui won, and Hafner finished last.

•   •   •   •   •

On another occasion Hafner wore a T-shirt that was lettered on the front: "I may not be very smart, but I can lift heavy things."

Mel Harder
(Pitcher, 1928-1947; coach, 1948-1963)

Before he died in 2002, Mel Harder said, "The biggest thrill of my baseball career was to pitch the first game ever played in Municipal Stadium [on July 31, 1932,] against Lefty Grove and the Philadelphia Athletics in front of [80,284] people. I would've liked to win, but I wasn't any more disappointed [to lose 1-0] than any game I lost.

"In all the [20] years I pitched in the major leagues, including the years I coached, I'd have to say another one of my favorite memories was the day [in 1928] that I met Connie Mack [who was both the owner and manager of the Philadelphia Athletics]. I was an 18-year-old kid, a rookie, and our manager, Roger Peckinpaugh, took me over to the Philadelphia dugout and introduced me to Mr. Mack.

"It was such a big thrill for me because he was such a great man. I pitched in relief against the Athletics that day, and it was in that game that Ty Cobb hit the last home run of his career, the only home run he hit all season. It also was the first home run I gave up in my career, which is another reason I remember the game so well."

•   •   •   •   •

Because he played a long time, from 1938 to 1947, with Lou Boudreau, Harder often was asked to compare him with Omar Vizquel.

"All I can say," Harder would reply, "is that Vizquel is a great shortstop, but for my money, I like Boudreau better.

"Lou was a very good offensive player and had great range defensively. He could field a grounder between shortstop and third base or one between shortstop and second base as well as anybody I ever saw. He also was very smart, very instinctive in the way he played the hitters, and when he teamed up with second baseman Ray Mack [1939-1946], they were the best double-play combination I ever saw. You had to see them to believe how good they were."

•   •   •   •   •

"One of the best players I played with was Earl Averill [from 1929 to 1939], who had a Hall of Fame career but one that almost ended in 1935 because of an accident with a firecracker.

"It happened during an off day and Averill, [Joe] Vosmik, myself, and our families went out in the country for a picnic. Somebody had some firecrackers, and Averill lit one and threw it, but it didn't go off. So he went out to pick it up, and just as he did, it exploded. At first we were afraid it blew a couple of fingers off his hand. Fortunately it didn't.

"Vosmik and I rushed Averill to the hospital, and though he turned out to be OK, it took him a while to get over his sore hand. He missed a lot of games [14], and his average fell to .288. It was the first season [in seven] that Averill didn't hit .300, although he came back the next year and was as good as ever [batting .378 in 1936, .299 in 1937, and .330 in 1938]."

Ken "The Hawk" Harrelson
(First baseman and outfielder, 1969-1971)

When he was traded to the Indians on April 19, 1969, Ken Harrelson initially refused to report to Cleveland, insisting he would retire.

"It was quite an experience," he said, "I held out for a week, although I wasn't holding out just for money. There were a couple of issues involved. Money was a non-issue at the time. I either got it, the salary I wanted [and a couple other concessions he was unwilling to specify], or I wasn't going to go to Cleveland.

"I finally got what I wanted and signed. Actually, the big reason I agreed was because of [then-Tribe manager] Alvin Dark and [catcher] Duke Sims. They were great friends of mine. I played for Alvin in Kansas City, and he always treated me great and gave me good advice. And Duke and I used to run together. We had a lot of fun. That's when we were young.

"I moved into the Winton Place when I got to Cleveland, and my apartment, which was on the top floor, overlooked the lake. It was beautiful. Art Modell had a place in the building, and so did Vernon Stouffer, and my place was nicer than theirs. My late sister Iris, who had an IQ of about 170, decorated the apartment, and it was unbelievable what she did.

"*Sports Illustrated* did a big layout on it. It was what you'd call the *consummate bachelor pad* because it had everything a bachelor could want in an apartment. A lot of mirrors, a lot of zebra skin, even a swing from the ceiling, although that was just for show.

"Every now and then, if I got hung up and it wasn't comfortable to go where I wanted to go, I could call up a helicopter to come and land on the roof of the building, and to get to it, all I had to do was walk up one flight of stairs.

"And, yes, I used it quite often.

"Now I look back on those days and just shake my head because it was—well, I'm a lot older and about 180 degrees different now than I was then. Actually, I don't think about those days unless somebody asks me, and it's hard for me to believe that I really did some of the things I did back then. I had fun, don't get me wrong, and it was all innocent fun, but I can't believe some of the things I did.

"Older conservative people didn't like me; I know that because I used to get mail all the time saying I should cut my hair, that I was a bad influence on kids. Occasionally I'd write back and say, 'Look, if your kid had a nose as big as mine and ears as big as mine, you'd let him wear long hair, too.'"

Ron Hassey
(Catcher, 1978-1984)

Although he is the only player in the history of base-ball to catch two perfect games in the major leagues, Ron Hassey said that the "highlight" of his career was "just being called up to the big leagues and to get my first hit off Dennis Eckersley in my first game. You don't forget things like that.

"Of course, I'll never forget catching those perfect games [by Lenny Barker in 1981] and Dennis Martinez [in 1991], but the highlight was just getting to the big leagues."

George Hendrick
(Outfielder, 1973-1976)

During his 18 seasons in the major leagues from 1971 to 1988—with Oakland (1971-1972), the Indians, San Diego (1977-1978), St. Louis (1978-1984), Pittsburgh (1985), and California (1985-1988)—George Hendrick earned the nickname, "Silent George," because of his unwillingness to be interviewed by the media.

Now the batting coach for the top farm club of the Los Angeles Dodgers, Las Vegas of the Class AAA Pacific Coast League, Hendrick realizes he was wrong.

"I guess part of the problem was that I was very young and didn't know how to handle it, the attention and all that stuff," Hendrick said during a recent return to Cleveland for a reunion with his former teammates.

"Right after I came to the Indians I was interviewed by a writer from Dallas after I'd had a pretty good game against [Texas Rangers pitcher] Lloyd Allen," he said. "I was quoted saying some pretty nasty things about Allen, things that I didn't say. I apologized to Allen and found out that he and the writer didn't get along, and that the writer used me to put Allen down.

"I decided then that I wouldn't trust anybody in the media, and the way I handled it was to not speak, not even to say hello. I was rude ... and I'm sorry now."

Chuck Hinton
(Outfielder, 1965-1967, 1969-1971)

Of his career in Cleveland, when the Indians played at the old Municipal Stadium, Chuck Hinton said, recalling a bad game he played against the Minnesota Twins in 1966, "You've never heard booing until you've been booed by 66,000 fans, although it was seldom that we had that many in the old Stadium.

"Then again, you've never heard cheering like when it comes from 66,000 fans, so I guess that evens it out, although, again, more times—*many more* times—than not, we didn't have 66,000 fans in the Stadium cheering or booing us."

Harold "Gomer" Hodge
(First, second, and third baseman, 1971)

He signed for a $1,000 bonus in 1963 and, when he made it with the Indians in 1971, after eight years in the minor leagues, his salary was all of $13,500 which, to Harold Hodge—better known as "Gomer"—was a lot of money.

For that matter, it still is, because the one-time utility infielder is drawing unemployment checks in his hometown of Rutherfordton, North Carolina. After ending his major league playing career of one season, Hodge played, coached, and managed in the minor leagues, as well as in Mexico and even Australia.

"I spent 39 years in professional baseball. It has meant everything to me. I want to stay in the game, but it is very hard to get a job," he said after his contract wasn't renewed as batting coach for Boston's Class AAA farm club, Pawtucket of the International League in 2001.

"I loved the game and the people in it, but it's all changed. Now it's all about money."

• • • • •

The "secret" to the minimal success he enjoyed with the Tribe in 1971, when he batted .205 with one homer in 80 games, Hodge said: "I asked the good Lord for help every time I went to the plate, and He helped me."

Willis Hudlin
(Pitcher, 1926-1940)

In 1936, at the height of his pitching career with the Indians, Willis Hudlin suffered a sore arm.

"In those days if you had a sore arm, the first thing doctors would tell you were to have your tonsils taken out," said Hudlin, who died in 2002. "They figured that tonsils absorbed poison and then the poison would get distributed to the part of your body you used the most, which for a pitcher was his arm.

"So, that winter [1936-1937] I had my tonsils removed and, sure enough, my arm was better in 1937. Was it because I had my tonsils taken out? I don't know. I was just glad that my arm felt better, never mind why."

He compiled a 158-156 won-lost record during his 16-year major league career, all but one season with the Tribe.

• • • • •

Early in Hudlin's career, on August 11, 1929, he made a pitch that wound up flying high and far over the right-field wall at League Park, which then was the Indians home field, after it was hit.

"In my mind I can still see the ball flying over that damned fence," Hudlin said in an interview many years later.

The ball that flew over that "damned fence" was hit by Babe Ruth and was the Bambino's 500th career homer, then the most hit by any player in baseball.

"My best pitch was a sinker, and that's what the Babe hit, although I guess that sinker didn't sink the way it was supposed to sink."

Luis Isaac
(Coach, 1994-)

"In the [11] years I've been a coach for the Indians, there are only two moments I'd like to forget," said Luis

Isaac, who's been employed by the organization longer than anyone presently on the staff.

It's not difficult to guess those two moments.

"One," he said, "was the sixth game of the 1995 World Series" when the Atlanta Braves beat the Indians 1-0 for the championship.

"The other, and I won't say which was worse, was the 11th inning of the seventh game of the 1997 World Series" when the Indians lost to the Florida Marlins 3-2.

"Both were hard," said Isaac, the Indians' Good Guy award winner in 1998.

David Jacobs
(Co-owner with brother Richard Jacobs, 1986-1992)

During their negotiations to buy the Indians in 1986 and after the purchase was finalized, the Jacobs brothers seldom met with, or spoke to the media, staunchly maintaining a strict code of privacy, especially the younger brother, Richard.

However, on one occasion during the winter of 1986-1987, David (who died in 1992), upon being congratulated during a social gathering by a man he had not yet met, spoke eloquently of the brothers' plans to build a winning team.

Upon the conclusion of David's remarks, the man to whom he'd been talking introduced himself as a reporter for *The Plain Dealer*.

Jacobs stammered, 'Oh, my goodness ... everything I told you is off the record ... off the record ... absolutely off the record, do you understand?"

The reporter acquiesced, albeit reluctantly—and several years later David Jacobs's "off the record" prophecy became true because the Indians won five consecutive division championships from 1995 to 1999, another in 2001, and pennants in 1995 and 1997.

Charley Jamieson
(Outfielder, 1919-1932)

After Charley Jamieson was honored with a "day" in 1929 and given a purse of $3,200, he grounded out to end the game as the Indians lost to future Hall of Famer Lefty Grove and the Philadelphia Athletics.

Jamieson, who died in 1969, sought Alva Bradley, then-owner of the Indians, and reportedly told him, "Mr. Bradley, I'm Scotch and I like money as well as the next guy. But I'd have given this whole $3,200 for one more hit off that big monkey."

Mike Kekich
(Pitcher, 1973)

Mike Kekich, who was notorious for trading wives, families, and homes (even dogs) with Fritz Peterson in 1972, before both players were acquired in separate transactions by the Indians, didn't last long, nor do well for the Tribe. After one season in Cleveland, Kekich was jettisoned to Texas and, subsequently, elsewhere, later claiming he was "blackballed" by major league teams.

Whether it was true or not, Kekich—who was once called "another Sandy Koufax" when he was a rookie with

Los Angeles in 1965—wound up pitching in the Mexican League.

When asked what it was like to play south of the border for Nuevo Laredo, Kekich described it this way: "We had 18- to 24-hour bus rides. There were spiders, cockroaches, and no air-conditioning in our motel rooms, the bed sheets just split from your weight, and the towels shredded when you touched them.

"When guys go to Mexico or Japan, they're usually never heard from again."

And Kekich never was.

Jim Kern
(Pitcher, 1974-1978, 1986)

When he attempted to make a comeback with the Indians in 1986 at the age of 37, Jim Kern, who, because of his appearance was nicknamed by his teammates, "The Emu," was quoted as saying, "My game is power. ... I'm strictly a one-trick pony."

However, Kern's comeback as a one-trick pony didn't last long. He was released 10 weeks into the season with a 1-1 won-lost record and 7.90 earned run average (with 11 strikeouts in 27⅓ innings on a yield of 34 hits, 28 runs, one homer, and 23 walks).

"I'm totally embarrassed by my statistics," he said when the end came. "I feel like somebody has been sticking needles in a voodoo doll of me. This is my fourth pink slip in the last three years, but I'm going to stick around long enough to get a whole deck.

"There's only one problem. I'm still throwing good, but I'm running out of teams."

Wayne Kirby
(Outfielder, 1991-1996)

When the Indians vacated Municipal Stadium at the end of the 1994 season and moved into Jacobs Field, Wayne Kirby had the perfect description for the switch.

"We went from the outhouse to the penthouse," he said.

Duane Kuiper
(Second baseman, 1974-1981)

Nobody ever considered Duane Kuiper to be a power hitter—of all the players in baseball history who had at least 3,000 plate appearances, he hit only one homer in his 3,379 at-bats while compiling a .271 career batting average in 12 seasons.

Kuiper's sole homer was slugged on August 29, 1977, against Steve Stone of the Chicago White Sox at the old Cleveland Stadium.

But the former Tribe second baseman who is now a broadcaster for the San Francisco Giants, shares a distinction as being one of only three players to hit two bases-loaded triples in the same game.

He did it on July 27, 1978, against rookie Bob Kammeyer of the New York Yankees in the first and fifth innings of the second game, a 17-5 Indians victory. It put Kuiper in the record book along side Elmer Valo of the Philadelphia Athletics, who tripled twice in a game in

1949, and Billy Bruton of the Milwaukee Braves, who did it in 1959.

"The Indians didn't have a weight room when I played. But if they had, maybe I would have developed more power," Kuiper quipped during a recent return to Jacobs Field. (Probably not.)

Frank Lane
(General manager, 1957-1961)

Because of his penchant for wheeling and dealing, Frank Lane was not a very popular man among Indians players. However, one who liked him a lot was Hal Naragon, who caught for the Indians in 1951 and again from 1954 to 1959, before he also was traded to Washington by Lane.

"During spring training in 1959, when my daughter Pam was about two years old, my wife, Joanne, often brought her to the ballpark to pick me up after a workout or exhibition game," Naragon recalled. "Somebody on the team that year had a big boxer dog, and my daughter loved to play with it. She loved dogs, still does.

"Lane really took a liking to Pam, and one day he came into the clubhouse and told me, 'Hal, since your daughter likes that dog so much, you go out and buy her one and I'll pay for it. Just send me the bill.' I told him, 'Frank, my wife travels so much with a two-year-old, and I don't think she could also handle a dog.' He said, 'Well, whenever the time comes that she can, you buy your daughter a dog and send me the bill.'

"So what happened? Lane traded me [on May 25, 1959], to Washington, and shortly after I left the Indians he sent me a letter. It said, 'I'm still waiting for that bill, because I still want to buy your daughter a dog.'

"A couple of months later I did. I paid $100 for a little poodle, and I sent him the bill, not really expecting I'd hear from him, but I did. He sent me a check for $100 with a nice little note.

"I know most guys didn't have good things to say about Lane, but I'm not one of them."

Matt Lawton
(Outfielder, 2002-2004)

"I was really scared when I got drafted by Minnesota [in 1991] and [Twins scout] Cal Ermer came to sign me," Matt Lawton reminisced about his start in professional baseball. "I didn't know if I wanted to go to college or what, so I didn't sign right away. South Alabama [University] was close to home, and I really didn't want to leave home, so I kept telling Mr. Ermer that I didn't think I wanted to play professional baseball."

But Ermer was persistent.

"I remember the last time he came to visit me, he brought his wife along and she got to talking to my mother. As it turned out, Mrs. Ermer persuaded my mother that, if I signed with the Twins, everything would be OK—which it turned out to be. And now, every time I see Mr. Ermer I thank him for giving me the opportunity, although I should thank his wife, too.

"I don't know what she said to my mother. You know women kind of bond together, and if she hadn't convinced my mother to let me sign, who knows what I'd be doing today, instead of working on my 10th year in the major leagues. My brother Marcus also played [10 games] in the major leagues for the New York Yankees."

•   •   •   •   •

The highlight of Lawton's amateur baseball career, he said, was in 1984 when he played second base and his double-play partner was shortstop Brett Favre, who went on to become an All-Pro NFL quarterback for the Green Bay Packers.

•   •   •   •   •

During the 2003 season when the Indians' roster was loaded with rookies, Lawton was not in the starting line-up.

"It's hard to say you get left out on a team as bad as ours," he said then. "I mean, if you can't play for a team this bad, who can you play for?"

Lawton made a "comeback" with the Indians in 2004 and became a very popular player in Cleveland. He was particularly upset midway through the 2003 season when, prior to a game at Jacobs Field as members of the Indians greeted fans as they entered the park, Lawton was approached by a little old lady.

"She must have been 100," Lawton said, "and she told me, 'I boo you every time you come to the plate, and I hope you start hitting so they can get rid of you.'"

So how did Lawton respond?

"What could I say to her. I just stood there, speechless, while she walked away. It was not a good time for me."

He was traded to Pittsburgh in the winter of 2004-2005.

Bob Lemon
(Outfielder, third baseman, and pitcher,
1941-1942, 1946-1958)

Before he became a full-time starting pitcher, Bob Lemon—who was elected in 1976 to the Hall of Fame—was hanging on with the Indians as an outfielder–third baseman who also made 32 pitching appearances, mostly in mop-up relief assignments in 1946.

In fact, in the 1946 opening game, Lemon made a sensational game-saving catch in center field to preserve Bob Feller's 1-0 victory over the Chicago White Sox, although it was the only high point of his outfield career. In 55 games that season Lemon batted .180 (16 for 89) and was 4-5 in 94 innings on the mound.

A year later, still without a regular position or even a defined role on the team, Lemon almost was lost in a waiver deal with the then-Washington Senators in a story related by Al Lopez, who was then a backup catcher for the Tribe.

"A lot of people probably find this hard to believe, but Bill Veeck tried to get rid of Lemon," Lopez said. "Veeck thought that Lemon would never hit enough to play either the outfield or third base, which probably was accurate, and until then nobody gave much thought to making him a starting pitcher.

"Midway through 1947, Veeck requested waivers on Lemon, and he was claimed by Washington. The day it happened I was playing golf with Lemon, Ken Keltner, and Joe Gordon, and when we got to the turn [the tee on the 10th hole], there was a message for Lem to call home. He did, and when he came back to us he said, 'It looks like I'll be leaving you guys. ... I'm going to Washington.' He was happy about the deal because he wanted to play and knew he wouldn't get much of a chance with us because we had Keltner at third and a veteran outfield. We finished the golf game, and he went home to pack.

"But what happened was that Veeck got mad at [Senators owner] Clark Griffith because [Griffith] prematurely announced the sale in the evening papers in Washington. Veeck said he owed Cleveland's morning paper [*The Plain Dealer*] the release, and called off the deal [before it was officially filed with the league office]. Imagine if the deal had gone through. The Indians would have missed a helluva pitcher.

"A few days later Bill McKechnie, who was one of [Tribe manager] Lou Boudreau's coaches, came to me and asked if I thought we should give Lemon a chance to concentrate on pitching?

"I told him, '[Lemon] is a good athlete, he's got a good arm and a helluva live fastball, but he's got to concentrate on his control, on getting the ball over the plate, and to develop a curveball and slider.' Actually, Lemon already had a pretty good slider that was better than most pitchers'

Bob Lemon unwinds in the locker room after a game. Hy Peskin/Time Life Pictures/Getty Images

curveballs because it broke so much … almost, in fact, too big [a break] for a slider."

Boudreau agreed to give the strong-armed outfielder a shot as a full-time starting pitcher through the second half of the 1947 season. And with Lopez and pitching coach Mel Harder working with Lemon, he went on to post an 11-5 record and 3.44 earned run average, with six complete games in 37 appearances—15 as a starter. And in 1948, when the Indians won the pennant and World Series, Lemon became a 20-game winner (20-14) and went on to win 20 in six of the next eight seasons.

"That's how lucky the Indians were," Lopez said. "There they were, on the verge of giving Lemon away for the waiver price. And if he'd gone to Washington, he would have ended up being an outfielder, just a mediocre outfielder at best."

Instead he became a Hall of Fame pitcher.

•　•　•　•　•

When asked if he took any bad games home with him, Lemon replied, "Never. I always left them in a bar along the way."

And these Lemonisms:

"The two most important things to a pitcher are good friends and a strong bullpen, and not necessarily in that order."

"Baseball was made for kids. … Grownups only screw it up."

Joe Lis
(Outfielder, 1974-1976)

"Now that I have my pension [vested], I can go to heaven or hell and Joey, [my son], and Susie, my wife, will still be taken care of," said Joe Lis, who never was a fan of Frank Robinson, who managed the Indians from 1975 to 1977.

"Superstars never make good managers, and maybe I'm fortunate because I've never been in that class. I've been up and down. I've gone through success and failure. When a guy did something wrong, Frank couldn't understand it because he always did things right.

"Not me. I've done a lot of things wrong."

Al Lopez
(Catcher and manager, 1947, 1951-1956)

"For me, 1954 was the greatest season in the world, but the way it turned out it also was my greatest disappointment," said Al Lopez, who turned 96 on August 20, 2004, and is the oldest living member of the Baseball Hall of Fame.

When asked why the Indians, who'd won a then-American League-record 111 games under Lopez, were swept by the then-New York Giants in the 1954 World Series, Lopez said, "I still don't understand. I still believe we were the better team. In fact, I believe that team was one of the best in the history of baseball, primarily because of our pitching staff."

That pitching staff featured a starting rotation of Early Wynn, Bob Lemon, Mike Garcia, and Art Houtteman. Bob Feller, nearing the end of his career, was the fifth starter, and the bullpen was headed by Ray Narleski and Don Mossi, and included Hal Newhouser, who also was nearing the end of his career.

Wynn and Lemon, each of whom won 23 games in 1954; Feller (13-3); and Newhouser (7-2 in relief) are in the Hall of Fame.

"If the Series had opened in Cleveland, we would have done better. We would have won the first game, maybe the first two games, because those two home runs that Dusty Rhodes hit were just little pop flies down the right-field line that wouldn't have gone out of the Cleveland Stadium," Lopez continued.

And as for the "greatest ever" catch Willie Mays made in the opener of the Series, robbing Vic Wertz of what would have been a homer in any major league ballpark other than the Polo Grounds, Lopez laughed and said: "It was a great catch, but the greatest? Willie made it more difficult than it actually was. He overran the ball and let it get over his head. He could have caught the ball to the side a lot easier than he did."

• • • • •

When Lopez managed the Chicago White Sox (from 1957-1965 and 1968-1969), he admitted he didn't appreciate the promotions that then-owner Bill Veeck staged to bolster attendance.

Manager Al Lopez talks to pitcher Mike Garcia. Yale Joel/Time Life Pictures/Getty Images

"My job was to manage the club and win ball games. I guess some of Bill's promotions did some good, but a winning team was the best promotion."

One promotion in particular upset Lopez.

"Veeck had what he called a 'Circus Day' and had a bunch of elephants and clowns running around the ballpark, along with caged animals, lions and tigers, the whole damned circus. We must have lost the day before because I wasn't in real good humor, and one of the elephants laid one—you know, call it a 'pie,' or whatever—about this big," Lopez said, holding his hands a couple of feet apart. "There were flies swarming around it and, I'll be damned if I didn't almost step right in it, when I went out of the dugout. It was awful.

"Another time Veeck hired a helicopter that was going to land on the pitcher's mound. I didn't like that either, but Veeck had advertised it would happen and couldn't call it off. As the helicopter was getting ready to come down, the phone in the dugout rang and it was Eddie Short [then the White Sox publicity director]. He said, 'Al, you know who's going to land in that helicopter?' I told him I didn't, and he said, 'It's Satchel Paige.'

"But that part of it was a joke. Eddie knew I wouldn't take Paige even if I got fired. So I said to Short, 'You tell the guy who's flying that helicopter to be ready to get the hell out of there because if Satchel Paige gets out, I'm going to leave and not come back.

"Short laughed and when the helicopter landed, guess who got out? It was the midget, Eddie Gaedel, the guy Veeck hired to pinch hit when he owned the St. Louis Browns [in 1951]."

•   •   •   •   •

Would Lopez want to manage again?

"Sure, I would, if I were 30 years younger," he said. "But if I were 30 years younger there are a lot of things I'd like to be doing again.

"Could I [manage today's players]? Sure. It's all a matter of doing with what you've got."

•   •   •   •   •

"I played against and with so many great hitters; it's hard for me to pick one or two over the others. But I have to say that Ted Williams was one of the most complete hitters I ever saw, although I would say that Babe Ruth was the best overall player.

"You've got to figure [Ruth] was a great hitter, a home run hitter, and at the same time he was a great pitcher. He would have made it to the Hall of Fame as a pitcher. I don't say he was the greatest hitter, but I am saying he was the greatest player, all around. I'd have to rate Joe DiMaggio high up there, too, along with Rogers Hornsby—remember, he hit .440 and .420 a couple of times, and Ty Cobb, although I saw only a little of him.

"But this I know, it'd be hard for anybody to pick one of those guys as the best."

Lopez, a National League catcher for 18 seasons before joining the Indians as a backup receiver in 1947, said he didn't have many occasions to talk with Ruth, except when they played spring training exhibition games.

"Babe was one of those guys who'd show up, take batting practice, play the game, and never had much to do with other guys.

"Lou Gehrig was different. He was a very friendly guy. A nice guy. Everybody liked him. I remember a time we played the Yankees in Bradenton, [Florida], in 1939 when I was with the [Boston] Braves. Gehrig came up to the plate and said to me, 'Al, you've caught against me a lot of times. ... What do you think I'm doing wrong? I'm having a lot of trouble.' I told him, 'Lou, you're not snapping the bat the way you did. You're kind of just pushing at the ball, feeling for it,' and he said, 'That's the way it feels to me, too, but I don't know why.'

"What he didn't know at the time—nobody did— that he had something wrong with him. It was just coming on him then. When the Yankees got back to New York for the opening of the season, they had him examined and that's when they found out what was wrong."

Gehrig was diagnosed with amyotrophic lateral sclerosis (ALS)—a.k.a. Lou Gehrig disease—and played only eight games in 1939, ending his then-record streak of playing 2,130 consecutive games. He died on June 2, 1941.

• • • • •

Lopez's memories of Rocky Colavito and Herb Score also are vivid.

"I'll never forget one of the first games Rocky played for us in 1956," he recalled. "Somebody, I don't remember who it was, hit a grounder that went through [second baseman] Bobby Avila's legs. Rocky got the ball in right field, and when the base runner rounded second, Rocky cut loose and fired it to third base, but overthrew the third baseman. It hit the wall behind third base and bounced all the way back to the field and damned if it didn't go right through Avila's legs again. Now Rocky picked up the ball and started to throw it home and we're yelling from the dugout, 'Hold the ball, Rocky. Hold it!' It was the damnedest thing I ever saw."

As for Score, Lopez recalled, "I was the manager when the Indians signed Herb in 1952 out of high school in Lake Worth, [Florida], and brought him to Cleveland for a workout before he went to the minors. Mike McNally, who was the Indians' farm director, told Herb, 'Don't throw hard, just get good and loose. Lopez will come out in a few minutes, and we want him to see how you throw.'

"So when I got out on the field, Herb had been throwing to Birdie Tebbetts. I stood behind Score and asked him, 'Herb, do you want to cut loose?' and he said, 'Yes, that's what I've been waiting to do.' I told him, 'Go ahead, but don't hurt yourself. If you want to wait until tomorrow or the next day, it'll be OK.' But he said he was ready.

"With that he said to Birdie, 'Mr. Tebbetts, I'm going to let it out,' and Birdie said, 'You mean you haven't thrown hard yet?' Herb said he hadn't and with that, Tebbetts yelled over to [catcher] Joe Tipton, 'Hey, Joe, c'mon over here and catch this kid. I'm the next hitter [in batting practice].'

"So Tipton came over, picked up Birdie's glove, and yelled, 'OK, kid, let it come.' Herb fired his first pitch, and it went right over Tipton's head. He didn't even get a glove on it, and the ball hit the backstop. Joe turned pale. If it had hit him, it would have hit him right between the eyes and maybe killed him.

"Tipton yelled to Birdie, 'Tebbetts, you son of a bitch, you almost got me killed,' which he did, and Tebbetts started laughing like hell. Then Tipton got down in a catcher's crouch and told Score to throw another pitch. Herb did, and it hit Tipton right on the instep of his left foot. Now Tipton was jumping around in pain and was really mad at Tebbetts. Finally Jim Hegan came out and caught Score."

John Lowenstein
(Outfielder, 1970-1977)

When asked what he planned to do after he retired from baseball, Lowenstein said, "I'm going to be a [players'] agent and go to Taiwan and sign up all the Little League champions."

He didn't.

• • • • •

Reviewing his major league career, Lowenstein said, "I went from playing a lot, to playing a little, to being used sometimes, and to playing on a platoon basis, although instead of being called a *platoon player*, I preferred being called a *situation player*."

Rick Manning
(Outfielder, 1975-1983)

Rick Manning remembered how it was in the "bad old days" of Cleveland baseball.

"A lot of guys on the team wanted to be traded because they thought the Indians would never be a winning team," Manning said. "Not me. I was one of the few players who lived here year round. I wanted to stay here. I actually thought that one day we'd turn it around and win a pennant.

"In fact, most spring trainings I believed we had a chance to win the division. How dumb was that? We were playing in the East Division with Baltimore, New York, and Boston, and the truth be told, I had no clue back then.

"Something else I remember is how hard the game is to play, and that the further you get from it, the easier it looks."

• • • • •

Asked to comment on Sammy Sosa's use of a corked bat in 2003, Manning admitted that he used a corked bat a few times during his playing career.

"It didn't do me any good," said the lifetime .257 hitter. "Instead of blooping a single in front of an outfielder, the few times I tried [a corked bat] all it probably did was help me fly out to an outfielder."

• • • • •

After he was appointed the Tribe's base running and outfield coach (in addition to broadcasting games on television), Manning spent time in the batting cage in spring training learning to hit with a fungo bat.

"Buddy Bell was giving me lessons," he said. "It was embarrassing because I kept hitting the ball over the center-field fence."

He didn't do that too often against live pitching. In his 13-year playing career Manning hit 56 homers in 5,248 at-bats.

"When I was playing [for the Indians and Milwaukee Brewers from 1975-1987] and I'd see all those old guys in uniform, I'd say to myself, 'I'm not listening to that coach. What does he know?'

"Now I'm one of those old guys. I guess it's true, what goes around comes around."

Jeff Manto
(Outfielder, 1990-1991, 1997-1999)

The Indians never seemed to get enough of Jeff Manto—although it also seemed they could never make up their mind about the first baseman–third baseman–outfielder. He spent five tours of duty with the organization from 1990 to 1999.

Manto joined the Indians initially in a deal with the California Angels, was released in November 1991; was reacquired in a trade with Toronto in 1997; was released in April 1998; was re-signed as a free agent in June 1998; was released after the end of the 1998 season; was re-signed and recalled in June 1999; was let go in July 1999; and finally was re-signed as a minor league free agent in August 1999 and released at the end of the 1999 season.

"I never had a bad day in the major leagues, although I never had many of them [days in the major leagues]," he said. "I just appreciate the game, and I know it owes me nothing."

Charlie Manuel
(Coach, 1988-1989, 1994-1999; manager, 2000-2002)

"When I was a rookie with Minnesota in 1969, we were playing Chicago one night, and after the game I stopped at the bar in the hotel for a beer," Charlie Manuel recalled an incident that occurred early in his career. "A few minutes after I sat down this white-haired old guy sat down next to me and asked if I was a player. I told him I was, and we started talking baseball.

"After a little while, and about three beers later, he asked me if I knew Charlie Finley [then-owner of the Oakland Athletics who made his home in Chicago]. I told him no, but that I'd heard he was a real nutcase because he's got his players wearing white shoes, and green and white uniforms, and wants baseball to start using orange balls.

"The old guy just sat there and listened and finally he said to me, 'By the way, what's your name?' I told him, and then he introduced himself. 'I'm Charlie Finley,' he said, and I about died. But he just laughed and bought me another drink.

"After that, every year until he died [in 1997] Mr. Finley sent me a Christmas card. He was really a good guy."

•   •   •   •   •

"I was in Cleveland for 15 seasons and had a great time and a lot of good memories. But they kicked me out of the teepee and sent me home. I had too many chiefs and not enough Indians.

"I'm a baseball guy, but sometimes there are politics involved in being a manager, and I don't know how to play politics. Maybe I need to learn how to do that in order to be a manager again.

"I wouldn't mind managing in Japan again. I learned how to speak the language—the trouble is, I speak it with a Southern drawl."

●　　●　　●　　●　　●

When it was reported during the 2001 season that Tribe pitcher C.C. Sabathia was suffering a sore back, Manuel was asked, "Was it because he slept wrong?"—as Sabathia had said.

Manuel replied, "I don't know. I didn't sleep with him."

●　　●　　●　　●　　●

After Manuel was fired as manager of the Indians on July 10, 2002, former Indians slugger Jim Thome spoke up on his behalf.

"It was difficult to watch the heat Charlie took because I know how much, deep down, he cared," said Thome, who signed with Philadelphia in 2003 after becoming a free agent. "Charlie was out there working with us every day, trying to do the right things to make us better. He did a lot of things to help us, [but] I think his hands were tied.

"For what he had, I think he did a great job, I really do. I think he did a tremendous job. He's a great baseball man. You don't spend that long in baseball without being a good baseball man. The Indians are going to miss him a lot, more than people realize."

Tom McCraw
(First baseman, 1972, 1974-1975; coach, 1975, 1979-1982)

Tom McCraw was a close-up observer of Frank Robinson when the latter was named Major League Baseball's first black manager. McCraw also was a close friend and admirer of Robinson.

"Frank's Opening Day home run in 1975 was one of the most amazing things I've ever seen in baseball," McCraw said. "I felt it was destiny. ... I mean, here's a guy who's a player–manager, and he hits a home run in his first at-bat as baseball's first black manager. How can that be? That's what you call answering the call. It was like something scripted in Hollywood.

"I was coaching at first base when Frank connected off [New York Yankees right-hander] Doc Medich. I thought, 'How can you do anything better than that?' If somebody had bet me that he'd hit the ball out of the park in his first at bat, I'd have lost everything I own, because I would have bet it all that he couldn't do it. Who would have bet otherwise? Even a single or a double. But no. He hits a home run. The most glorified hit in the game. It's one of my favorite days in baseball."

• • • • •

It also was early in the 1975 season that Phil Seghi, then general manager of the Indians, was quoted as saying the team had a chance to win the pennant.

"I didn't say anything at the time, but I wondered what Phil was smoking in his pipe when he made that statement," McCraw recalled.

(The 1975 Indians finished fourth with a 79-80 record, 15½ games behind the Boston Red Sox.)

Sam McDowell
(Pitcher, 1961-1971)

Sam McDowell is the first to admit that he drank himself out of baseball and that he ruined what most observers believe would have been a Hall of Fame career.

Instead, his career ended in 1975, four years and three teams (San Francisco, New York Yankees, Pittsburgh) after being traded to the Giants for Gaylord Perry on November 29, 1971.

"Sudden Sam," as McDowell was nicknamed during his pitching career, has been sober for 16-plus years. But he also is the first to admit that his sobriety and his recovery from alcoholism is an ongoing day-to-day project.

"I am still an alcoholic. I always will be one; it's something that never changes," he said.

"I was a jerk, and I know it. But I also know it was alcoholism that made me a jerk. I don't like to talk about my career because I truly believe in my recovery. I live one day at a time, and I don't give a [bleep] about the past. I think about today and what I can do today to better myself as a person, what I can do today to help somebody else, what I can do today to try to do things the right way, that's all I care about. And if people don't like it, tough [bleep]."

When asked if he regrets not making it to the Hall of Fame and that his credentials—a 141-134 lifetime record for 15 major league seasons—fell far short of what so many had anticipated when he signed his first professional contract with the Indians in 1961, McDowell said:

"I would love to be in the Hall of Fame, but I know I would not be here today if it were not for my alcoholism and my subsequent recovery. ... I know I would not be here if I had not gone through the alcoholism and the recovery process. And I know, too, that I would not be in the position I'm in, or have the respect of my peers that I know I have, and the satisfaction of helping others who need the help that I can give, but couldn't get during my career in baseball.

"But that said, there also is absolutely no doubt in my mind that I would be in the Hall of Fame if I had not been a drunk, if I had not been kicked out of baseball because of my drinking. If I'd had the kind of help that I can provide players now, Nolan Ryan might not be baseball's leading strikeout pitcher."

Of his aborted career—aborted because of his drinking—McDowell said, "I was a very proud pitcher, very proud. That's the only reason I was a winner with a team like the Cleveland Indians. Not that they were bad guys, but we had no talent, and everybody knew it, and so did Gabe Paul. He was not trying to win a pennant. He was out to make money with the team, and that was it. He

Sam McDowell sits in the Indians dugout between innings. Art
Rickerby/Time Life Pictures/Getty Images

knew how to make it, no matter what. We knew we were going to be in last place when we left spring training.

"But I always tried hard, no matter what. I never wanted to be embarrassed on the mound, and I don't think I ever was. I always tried to give it everything I had out there."

Tom McGough
(Pitcher, 1977)

"It was spring training, 1976, in a Cactus League game against the San Francisco Giants in Phoenix that I had one of my most memorable baseball experiences," Tom McGough said. "My sole assignment for the afternoon, or so I thought, was simply to keep the pitching chart.

"But when Ray Fosse, who was rehabilitating an off-season knee surgery, came to the plate with two outs and nobody on base, the stage was set for my pinch running debut. [Manager] Frank Robinson looked at me and said, 'Mac, if Ray gets on, you're going to run for him.' At first I thought Frank was kidding. I was fast, and I always ran hard when we did wind sprints, but there is a big difference between that and being a base runner in a major league game.

"Well, Ray hit a sharp double, and sure enough, I got the nod from Robinson to 'get in there.' It wasn't until I was actually standing on second base and heard my name over the loudspeaker that I realized that I hadn't even been on the base paths since high school. Of course, I didn't even know the signs. But I've never been one to back away from a challenge, so I was determined to do my very best for the team.

"As Duane Kuiper, the next batter, stepped to the plate, I couldn't help but hope that he'd hit a home run so that I could just jog home. Instead, Kuip drilled a sharp single to right. I was moving on the pitch and got a good jump, but as I rounded third base [coach] Joe Nossek signaled for me to stop. Then, suddenly, both of us noticed the throw from right field was going to sail over the catcher's head, so I continued home, now believing there would be no play on me at the plate. What I didn't see was the pitcher, Bob Knepper, backing up the plate.

"He caught the wild throw and fired a perfect strike to catcher Mike Sadek, who faked me to perfection as I was just a few feet from home. My eyes were riveted on the plate until I noticed the catcher turning toward me with the ball in his glove. It was anything but pretty, but somehow I contorted to a degree that would have made Houdini proud, and—well, *sort of*—dived successfully over Sadek, eluding the tag and scoring the run.

"Needless to say my teammates were highly amused, but my rebuttal to this day remains in the simple fact that I was, albeit quite comically, 'safe at home.'

"Also, needless to say, I was never asked to pinch run for anybody again—which didn't bother me a bit."

Jose Mesa
(Pitcher, 1992-1998)

After ending his career with the Indians under less than friendly circumstances, Jose Mesa went on to pitch for San Francisco, Seattle, Philadelphia, and Pittsburgh. It was during the 2004 season, when Mesa regained his star status as a closer with the Pirates, that he was approached by a Cleveland sportswriter for an interview.

Before the scribe could even say hello, Mesa looked up and said, "Don't even ask," which ended the proposed interview before it even began.

Calvin McLish
(Pitcher, 1956-1959)

Cal McLish pitched for Brooklyn, Pittsburgh, Cincinnati, the Chicago White Sox, the Chicago Cubs, and Philadelphia, in addition to the Indians, during a 15-year major league career. He was never a 20-game winner—although he came close in 1959 with the Tribe.

That was the season the Indians almost won the American League pennant but were beaten in the final week by Chicago.

It also was the reason McLish still bears resentment toward Frank Lane, then-general manager of the Indians.

He recalled, "I'd won 19 games and was scheduled to start two days later, on Sunday in the final game of the season, which would give me a chance to win my 20th [against Kansas City, then one of the teams with one of the worst records in the league].

"But when I got to the clubhouse that Friday night, I was called into [manager] Joe Gordon's office. Lane was there with Gordon and [pitching coach] Mel Harder, and Lane said, 'Cal, would you mind giving up your start on Sunday so Herb Score could pitch?'

"Well, I wanted the chance to win my 20th, but I liked Herbie a lot. He was still trying to come back from that [1957] eye injury ... and I told Lane that I was willing to do it for Score's sake.

"What I didn't know, but found out later, was that Lane had already traded me to Cincinnati, even though it wasn't to be announced until later. That was the first year they had interleague trading and, naturally, if I had stayed and won 20, it would have been embarrassing for Lane.

"I found out about it after the season was over, when Hal Lebovitz called me and told me how it happened.

"So, in effect, while I thought I was giving up a chance to win 20 for Herbie, what I really did was give it up for Lane—which was really rotten of him. Absolutely rotten. I saw Lane once after that, but I didn't mention it. What good would that have done? It was too late to worry about it.

"I also thought it was rotten that Joe [Gordon] and Mel [Harder] didn't stick up for me. I kind of felt bad about that, too, but that's baseball. That's the way it is in baseball."

• • • • •

When asked about his given name(s)—Calvin Coolidge Julius Caesar Tuskahoma—McLish said, "It was my father who named me, but I don't know where the 'Calvin Coolidge' part of it came from. As far as I know my dad wasn't even a Republican. I guess he just liked the name, the same as he probably liked 'Julius Caesar.'"

As for "Tuskahoma," McLish said it was the name of a town in the Indian territory of Oklahoma where his parents were born.

"Dad was ¼ Chickasaw, and mom was ¹⁄₁₆ Cherokee, which makes me ⅛ Chickasaw and ¹⁄₃₂ Cherokee," said McLish, who also is part Scotch, English, Irish, and Dutch.

Al Milnar
(Pitcher, 1936, 1938-1943)

"The Indians called me in 1933 after I'd pitched well in an amateur league in Cleveland and invited me for a try-out," Al Milnar recounted the beginning of his professional baseball career. "They gave me a bonus for going to the tryout—a streetcar fare from my home [on Cleveland's East Side] to League Park. That was it."

Milnar, who still lives in Euclid, pitched for the Tribe as a reliever briefly in 1936 and all of 1938 and was a starter in 1939 and 1940, compiling a 32-22 won-lost record before suffering an injury early in the 1941 season.

"I hurt my shoulder throwing sliders, which at that time was a new kind of pitch," Milnar said. "Johnny Allen, [a former teammate], taught me how to throw it, but looking back at it I wish he hadn't. In those days the doctors didn't know what to do about a sore arm. They just rubbed it with alcohol, and if you complained too much, well it was 'Goodbye Charlie.'"

Milnar's record fell to 12-19 in 1941, and he never had a winning season thereafter, winding up with a 57-58 eight-year major league career record that included parts of

1943 and 1946 with the old St. Louis Browns and Philadelphia Phillies.

"Today, they can practically put a new arm on you and send you to the minor leagues for rehabilitation," Milnar said.

"But in my day you kept your mouth shut and didn't complain, or even say anything about a sore arm, because there always were a couple of guys on the bench ready to take your job. When my arm went bad, I just kept pitching, and my arm never got any better. It hurts me to this day.

"And we also weren't smart enough to hire agents in my day. But then, we didn't think we needed them. We felt lucky just to get a paycheck twice a month, and to play the game we loved."

Saturnino Orestes "Minnie" Minoso
(Outfielder, 1949, 1951, 1958-1959)

When Minnie Minoso played for the New York Cubans of the Negro National League in 1948, Joe Vosmik scouted the outfielder–third baseman for the Indians. In his report to then-owner Bill Veeck, Vosmik called Minoso "the fastest thing on legs," and the Tribe quickly purchased Minoso's contract for $25,000.

After Minoso joined the Dayton (Ohio) Indians of the Class A Central League for the final two weeks of the 1948 season, Vosmik's subsequent report was even more glowing as Minoso batted .525 in 11 games.

"[Minoso] can hit major league pitching right now—and if there is anything higher than major leagues, he'll hit that, too," Vosmik said.

• • • • •

In 1959 when Fidel Castro came to power in Cuba, the communist government seized Minoso's family's vast holdings in that country, leaving Minnie penniless. It was written that "an incalculable fortune was lost in a heartbeat," but Minoso refused to lament the loss.

"I come from the ranch," he explained. "I had one pair of shoes, but I had dignity because my mother and father gave me the idea that money wasn't everything."

• • • • •

Minoso "retired"—although he refused to use that word—in 1964 and managed and played in the Mexican League from 1965 to 1975. He was activated by the White Sox for three games in 1976 when he was 49 (or 52, depending upon whose records you believe) and returned again for two games in 1980 at the age of 55 (or 58), giving him five decades in the major leagues.

At the time he said, "I sometimes think I am dreaming, and I don't want to wake up. I want to stay in baseball the rest of my life."

He wanted to be activated again in 1990, for a record sixth decade, but then-commissioner Fay Vincent would not give his approval.

Terry Mulholland
(Pitcher, 2002-2003)

"It was during 1997 and 'Mo,' my nickname for Mulholland, was then pitching for San Francisco against the Phillies, one of Mulholland's former teams, in Philadelphia," recalled Joe Bick, a player agent for Mulholland. "He hit a home run—the ball was absolutely crushed and was measured at about 451 feet—which ended up being the second longest home run ever hit in Veterans Stadium that year.

"When the season was over, I was watching a game in the Arizona Fall League in Phoenix, where Mulholland lives. While we're sitting around shooting the bull one night I said, 'You know, 'Mo,' it amazes me that a guy who is as big and strong as you are and can hit a ball as far as you did in that game against the Phillies last season can't hit it a little more often.' He was a typical pitcher … you know, not much of a hitter.

"He said to me in all seriousness, 'Well, Joe, I think if you look back in the history of baseball you'd see that a number of premier power hitters never hit for much of an average.'

"And with that we both broke up."

•   •   •   •   •

In Terry Mulholland's perfect world he would start every fifth day and make two relief appearances in between.

"You have to understand," he said. "I love pitching, and I love playing baseball. I've been this way since I was six years old. There is nothing more gratifying than when a manager gives you a baseball and tells you to go get people out."

As for his advanced age (his birthdate is listed in *The Baseball Register* as March 9, 1963), Mulholland—who pitched for 10 major league teams, including Seattle and Minnesota in 2004 in a professional baseball career that began in 1984—said of himself, "I'm the youngest 41-year-old I know … and when I was 30, I was the youngest 30-year-old I knew."

Playing for a contract every year is not easy.

"It all depends on how much self-confidence you have and staying prepared to play baseball. You have to stay healthy, too," he says. "And don't complain about a lack of security [in baseball]. If you want security, learn how to work a monkey wrench."

•   •   •   •   •

In 2003, when he was both a starter and reliever for the Indians, Mulholland was called in to pitch in the middle of an inning when rookie Jason Davis was ejected from a game against Minnesota in mid-July. Although he was entitled to throw as many warmup pitches as he wanted, Mulholland took only eight and then promptly struck out Lew Ford on four pitches.

"That's the way you did it back home," Mulholland said. "You'd be playing right field in a summer league game, and they'd tell you to go in and pitch. Eight warmup pitches were all you got and all you needed.

"That's why big leaguers are such pansies. They're too coddled."

Former Indians pitcher Terry Mulholland was all about baseball on and off the mound. Rick Stewart/Getty Images

• • • • •

After pitching against—and beating the Indians—as a member of the Minnesota Twins on August 16, 2004, Mulholland said, "The thing I learned watching them is that you can't give them anything they can hit real hard. [So] I tried to tease them. Heck, I'll try anything. If I was allowed to take sandpaper to the ball, I'd do that."

Eddie Murray
(First baseman–designated hitter, 1994-1996; coach, 2002-)

During his induction speech at the Hall of Fame on July 27, 2003, as the 38th player elected on the first ballot, Eddie Murray said, "When Ted Williams was inducted 37 years ago, he said he must have earned it because he didn't win it because of his friendship with the writers.

"I guess in that way I'm proud to be in his company. I was never one much on words. I had a job to do. I'd seen people get caught up with doing well. I didn't want things like that to control me.

"For me, to focus a lot on the individual, that's not the way I learned to play the game. Baseball is a team game."

And to the youngsters in the audience during the Hall of Fame ceremonies, Murray said, "For every kid here today, I wish you could feel what I'm feeling, because I had a dream as a kid, and I actually lived that dream. It's unbelievable. I loved playing baseball. I still love this game."

Ray Murray
(Catcher, 1948, 1950-1951)

"[Hank] Greenberg was not one of my favorite people, even before he traded me away. I didn't hate the man, I just didn't like his attitude, his kind of B.S.," Ray Murray reflected on his brief career with the Indians.

"Greenberg always looked at me like I was some kind of trash, and we never saw eye to eye. He always wanted to be the big dog in everything. We never had much opportunity to talk, but if I had, I would have talked pretty plain to him.

"One time early in 1951 Greenberg came in the clubhouse and was popping off about someone. I said to him, 'If you feel that way, if you're going to talk about a guy that way, why the hell don't you get rid of him,' and right after that he got rid of me."

Murray was traded to the then-Philadelphia Athletics on April 30, 1951, in a three-team deal that brought pitcher Lou Brissie to Cleveland.

Hal Naragon
(Catcher, 1951, 1954-1959)

"It was 1955, my second full season with the Indians, and Hank Greenberg and I just couldn't get together on my contract," said Hal Naragon, talking about how different salary negotiations are today, compared to his era. "In those days management was in the driver's seat and players didn't have much leverage. Finally Hank said that if I was still on the club on June 15, he'd give me a $1,500 raise, so I signed.

"Then, sometime in May, we played the Yankees on a Friday night in front of a big crowd in the Stadium. Early Wynn pitched, and we won—and anytime we beat the Yankees it was a good game to win. I happened to get a hit or two and also, late in the game, I caught a foul ball down toward the third base line with men in scoring position. I called everybody off. ... I wouldn't let anybody catch it except me, and it helped us win.

"The next day I went into the clubhouse and was called up to Greenberg's office. I thought, uh-oh, maybe they're going to send me back to Indianapolis, which then was the Indians' top farm club.

"But Greenberg told me he liked that play I made— the way I took charge of the foul ball—and said, 'You know the deal we had, the $1,500 part of it?' I said, 'Yes, sir,' and he said, 'It's yours,' even though it was long before June 15 [and] before he had to give it to me or not."

• • • • •

One of Naragon's favorite teammates was Mike Garcia, who threw all the standard pitches—fastball, curve, slider, change-up—and, occasionally, a spitball.

"We were playing Boston at the Stadium, I think it was in 1955, and Ted Williams was batting against Garcia, who'd load up a pitch every once in awhile—and boy, he had a good one. He didn't load up many, but he did when he felt he needed it. And when he loaded one up, Mike would shake his head and his glove so I'd know to expect it.

"So this time Williams is at the plate, we've got two strikes on him, and I got down and gave Mike a signal. I don't remember what I called for, fastball or curve or whatever, but Mike shook his head and his glove to let me know he was loading one up.

"He threw it and—honest to God!—it was right down the middle, about knee high, and when it got to the plate, the ball dropped about a foot.

"But even before the pitch got to the plate, Williams yelled, 'There's something on that ball!' Honest, he did.

"Of course, a spitter, most of the time, doesn't have much rotation and isn't really thrown very hard, but for Williams to see something on the ball like he did was amazing.

"I caught the pitch—it was a ball because Williams didn't swing and it dropped out of the strike zone—and right away I threw it back to Mike. The umpire, Hank Soar, walked around in front of the plate and yelled to Mike, 'Throw me the ball,' and Mike rolled it on the ground to him,' which cleaned it up.

"Then Williams turned to me and said, 'What was that pitch, Hal?' and I said, 'It was a sinker,' and that was the end of it."

•   •   •   •   •

Another "amazing" story—one that's even so scary that Naragon admits he researched its accuracy—involved Early Wynn and former Indians outfielder Gene Woodling.

"During the 1951 season when Woodling was then with the Yankees, we played them on June 24 in New York. Early Wynn was pitching for us and the score was tied 3-3 going into the bottom of the eighth inning. Woodling came up and hit a two-run homer, and the Yankees beat us 5-3.

"Exactly a month later, on July 24, we were in New York again, Wynn was pitching again, and we were leading 2-0 in the sixth inning. Woodling came up and hit another two-run homer off Early, tying the score, and the Yankees eventually won 3-2.

"Then, which is even more amazing—and kind of *scary*, too, to tell the truth—a month after that, on August 24, we played the Yankees again and this time the game was scoreless in the eighth until Woodling, of course, hit another two-run homer off Wynn, and the Yankees won that game 2-0.

"All this happened on June 24, July 24, and August 24 of 1951—and to top it off, consider that Early Wynn's uniform number was 24.

"You could say that it was fortunate for the Indians—and especially Early—that September 24, 1951, was an open date for us."

· · · · ·

Indians pitchers of that era—the early to mid-1950s—were renowned as a fun-loving bunch, led by Bob Lemon and Early Wynn, which reminded Naragon of another story regarding his former batterymates.

"We were in Boston to play the Red Sox, when Lou Boudreau was their manager, and Al Lopez asked one of their writers who was pitching the next day. The writer said, 'We never know because Boudreau doesn't like to tell his pitchers when they are going to pitch because they'd get nervous and wouldn't have a good night's sleep.'

"Lopez said, 'Geez, I have to tell my pitchers so they *will* get a good night's sleep.'"

• • • • •

"Elroy Face had a terrific forkball [for Pittsburgh, Detroit, and Montreal from 1953 to 1969] that had made him a very successful relief pitcher, so good that he maybe should even be in the Hall of Fame.

"I knew him when I was a coach for the Tigers in 1968, which was about the time the split-fingered fastball—what they now call a *splitter*—was becoming very popular, and I asked him, 'What's the difference between the forkball that you threw and a splitter?'

"He said, 'Three million dollars.'"

Graig Nettles
(Third baseman, 1970-1972)

After he was traded by the Indians to the Yankees in 1973 and played for New York for 11 years during the Bronx Zoo days, Nettles remarked, "Some kids dream of joining the circus, others of becoming a Major League Baseball player. As a member of the New York Yankees, I've gotten to do both."

Hal Newhouser
(Pitcher, 1954-1955)

Here's how close Hal Newhouser, a Hall of Famer and one of baseball's all-time best pitchers, almost played for the Indians as a teammate of Bob Feller.

"A bird dog scout for the Indians saw me pitch an amateur game in 1938 and invited me to Cleveland for a tryout. They put me and my mother up in a hotel where Bob Feller was staying. They wanted me to meet him, but Bob was out and didn't get back by the time we had to leave.

"The next day I worked out at League Park. Steve O'Neill was the Indians manager then and told me, 'Kid, you've got a real good arm, take care of it,' but all they told me was that they'd stay in touch, so my mother and I went home [to Detroit].

"I didn't hear from the Indians again, at least not until it was too late, and I've often thought about what might have been.

"Wish Egan, the famous scout for the Tigers, came to my home with Del Baker, then a coach for the Tigers. Egan laid five $100 bills on the table and told my parents, 'This is a bonus that Harold can do anything he wants with it, and here's a contract for him to play in the minor leagues for $150 a month.'

"Remember, this was during the Depression and I was trying to earn money selling newspapers, making a half cent on each one; setting pins in a bowling alley; and collecting milk and pop bottles to get the deposit. My parents didn't have much money. Dad worked as a patternmaker in the automobile industry, and I was going to be a tool and die maker.

"So we signed the contract. I gave $400 to my parents and kept the other $100 for transportation and tuition to the trade school I was attending. I thought it was unbelievable that I would get so much money to play baseball.

"About 10 minutes after we signed the Tigers' contract, a big car pulled up in front of our house. It was a new Lincoln Continental. Two men got out and came to our door. One was Mr. Bracken, the Cleveland bird dog scout who'd seen me pitch on the sandlots, and the other was Cy Slapnicka, who was then the general manager of the Indians.

"Bracken said to my dad, 'Mr. Newhouser, here are the keys to that car out front. It's yours. And here's a check for $15,000 for Harold because we want to sign him. He will be Bob Feller's roommate, and we are going to have the two greatest young pitchers in baseball.'

"I looked at my parents and didn't know what to say. Neither did they. Finally I said, 'Mr. Bracken, I signed a contract with Detroit.' He said, 'When?' I told him, 'About 10 minutes ago.'

"With that, Slapnicka jumped out of his chair and yelled at Bracken, 'Damn you! If you hadn't insisted that we stop and pick up that car, we would have been here first.'

"With that, they left. I'm not sure if Slapnicka was angrier than the frustration my parents and I felt, but what could we do? I had signed with the Detroit Tigers and was a member of their organization."

• • • • •

Feller and Newhouser started against each other 19 times. Feller won 13, Newhouser won three, and three other decisions were credited to relief pitchers.

"We really brought the fans out when we pitched against each other, and I'd love to see something like that happen in baseball again," Newhouser said. "We were both tough competitors, but there never was any animosity between us.

"Ironically, in 1946, when Feller broke Rube Waddell's season strikeout record, he put me in the book with him. I was Bob's record-breaking victim—but I still think I was called out on a bad pitch. Not only was it out of the strike zone, it also was high. All hell broke loose in the stands when the umpire called me out.

"I was peeved at my teammates, because none of them wanted to be the one to strike out and give Feller the record. They were more concerned about *not* striking out than winning the game. I overheard some of them talking on the bench, saying things like, 'I'm going to swing at the first pitch because I'm not going to let [Feller] get two strikes on me.'

"After I struck out I went back to the dugout and said, 'Are you guys satisfied that it wasn't you? Now can we go out and win the damn game?'

"The reason I was so upset was that I had an agreement with the general manager that I would get back the 25-percent salary cut I had taken the year before. But I never got it. I won only 17 and lost 17 that season."

Phil Niekro
(Pitcher, 1986-1987)

"I'm sick of hearing I'm 47 years old," Phil Niekro said when he was acquired by the Indians in a waiver deal on April 3, 1986. "Everybody has to have a birthday. Somebody has to be the oldest player in baseball, and somebody has to be the youngest.

"I just happen to be the oldest ... so give it a rest. Stop writing how old I am."

• • • • •

And when Niekro pitched the Indians to a 9-6 victory over Detroit on June 1, 1987, Phil and his younger brother Joe became the winningest brothers in Major League Baseball. They had a combined total of 530 victories, 314 for Phil and 216 for Joe, which was one more victory than the Perry brothers achieved—314 for Gaylord and 215 for Jim.

Jesse Orosco
(Pitcher, 1989-1991)

"At last count I've pitched in 41 ballparks," said Jesse Orosco, who finally retired in 2004 at the age of 47 after a 25-year career in professional baseball. "My favorite park always was Camden Yards in Baltimore. And my least favorite always was Municipal Stadium [in Cleveland]. Because it was so old, there always were so few fans, and it always seemed to be drizzly and cold."

Tony Peña
(Catcher, 1994-1996)

It was the highlight of Tony Peña's 18-year major league playing career—his two-out solo home run off Zane Smith in the 13th inning of the first game of the 1995 American League Division Series. It enabled the Indians to beat Boston 5-4, propelling them to three straight victories

Phil Niekro was the oldest player in baseball when he was acquired by the Indians in 1986. Gray Mortimore/Getty Images

into the League Championship Series and, ultimately, the World Series.

Peña's home run has been voted by Tribe fans as the most memorable moment in the 10-year history of Jacobs Field.

What most fans didn't realize—and which never was made public until Peña, as the manager of the Kansas City Royals admitted it during the 2004 season—was that he ignored a "take" sign by then-third base coach Jeff Newman on the pitch that he hit into the left-field bleachers for the game-winning homer.

The count on Peña, leading off the 13th inning, was three and zero.

"I didn't see [Newman's take sign]," he said. "I just saw the pitch and swung. Then I saw the ball go over the wall. Then I saw everybody waiting for me at home plate. It was the most beautiful moment ever.

"It was a moment I'm never going to forget, and nobody is going to take away from me. Actually, it wasn't just the best moment in this ballpark or the best moment I had with the Indians. It was the best moment of my career."

And this final clarification by Mike Hargrove, then the Indians manager. When Peña said he didn't see Newman's sign, Hargrove smiled and said, "Well, at first I gave the take sign, but maybe I took it off. ... I just don't remember."

Gaylord Perry
(Pitcher, 1972-1975)

"You have to do what you have to do [to win]," Gaylord Perry always said when asked about charges that he threw illegal spitballs—or, more specifically, in his case, illegal "greaseballs"—although he never really denied it or admitted it.

"I just loved to make [opposing batters] *think* I was loading one up," he said.

When pointedly asked if he did indeed throw spitters or greaseballs, Gaylord chuckled and replied, "I always felt, and still do, that it's something for me to know and for the hitters to think about.

"I especially loved to pitch against the Yankees, because they were so easy to get going. With guys like Bobby Murcer and Reggie Jackson, all you had to do was put the thought [of a spitball] in their mind.'"

Murcer always insisted that Perry was a "cheater" despite Perry's claims that he was throwing a forkball and not a spitter. The former Yankees center fielder once said, "The only absolutely unhittable pitch I've seen in my whole career was Gaylord's hard spitter and, dammit, it wasn't a forkball."

And to keep the controversy alive in Murcer's mind, one Christmas Gaylord sent the outfielder a gallon of lard as a present.

Another who was really spooked by Perry was former Boston outfielder Fred Lynn. After going zero for four against Perry in a game in 1973, Lynn cursed Gaylord and said, "I saw only two pitches from Gaylord all night that were legal. He calls that thing a forkball, but there ain't a forkball alive that does what that thing does."

Once, in 1982 when he pitched for Seattle, Perry was ejected from a game by umpire Dave Phillips but insisted he was innocent, at least that time … that he was a victim of circumstances.

"We were getting beat by California and [Mariners manager] Rene Lachemann wasn't very happy," Perry said. "I didn't have much that day, and late in the game the Angels loaded the bases and Lynn, who was playing for California then, was the next batter. Lachemann came to the mound and told me, 'Dammit, Gaylord, put something on the ball.' He meant I should throw the ball hard, you know, that I should bear down, and I guess Phillips heard him.

"When my next pitch sunk about two feet, Phillips came running out from behind the plate screaming, 'You're out of here!' All I could say was, 'Thanks a lot, Lach.'"

After he was ejected by Phillips, Perry said he took a polygraph test and passed it with flying colors.

"F. Lee Bailey, the famous lawyer, gave me the test on a television program that was called *Lie Detector*. He asked me, 'Gaylord, did you put anything on the ball in the fifth inning of that game you were thrown out of?' and I said, 'No, I did not,' and I passed."

After he retired from baseball in 1984, Gaylord made a "fun video," as he called it. "It's about a [fictional] minor league ball team called the San Clemente Bulldogs that's losing every game by five or six runs. The coach gets mad because he wants to work his way up to the major leagues, but his team is doing so bad. So he tells them, 'I'm sending you to a baseball camp,' which is really the 'Gaylord Perry Baseball Camp.'

"They come and I teach them all these tricks, and they go back to San Clemente. Tricks, you know, like how to throw a spitter, scuff baseballs, cork bats, how to disguise them, how to hold on to a guy's belt when he's trying to get a lead off base.

"You know, all the things they do in the big leagues."

Did he teach the players how to throw "greaseballs"?

"Oh, no," he deadpanned. "I showed 'em how to *look* like they were loading up, how to make batters think things that bother them the way I bothered Bobby Murcer and Reggie Jackson. Remember? But you also should remember, none of those guys—Murcer, Jackson ... all the others who accused me of cheating—didn't accuse me of throwing an illegal pitch when they hit a home run off me."

•　•　•　•　•

"I know a lot of guys on my team didn't like me too much because I pushed them. A great example involved Buddy Bell when he first came up. He was a third baseman, but we had Graig Nettles so [manager] Ken Aspromonte put him in the outfield, and one day a guy hit a ball to center field. Buddy went back to the fence, jumped up, and got his glove on the ball, but instead of catching it, it got away and fell over the fence for a home run.

"When the inning was over I was waiting for him in the dugout. I'm teed off and said to him. 'You don't have to help those guys. They get enough runs without you making it easier for them,' and Buddy said, 'Well, then, don't let them hit the ball so hard.'

"That got me instant respect for Buddy because he was right. I shouldn't have let the guy hit the ball so hard, and I knew right then and there I didn't have to push him anymore."

Dave Philley
(Outfielder, 1954-1955)

"There's only one way to play this game … you've got to bleed and believe," said Dave Philley, who was one of 10 surviving players of the 1954 American League champion Indians who were honored in 2004 in observance of the golden anniversary of that team.

Other surviving members of the 1954 team that won a then-record 111 games: Bob Feller, Bill Glynn, Don Mossi, Hal Naragon, Ray Narleski, Rudy Regalado, Al Rosen, George Strickland, and Wally Westlake, and manager Al Lopez.

Boog Powell
(First baseman, 1975-1976)

When Boog Powell returned to Cleveland for an old-timers game in 1991 and was issued the all-red—jersey and pants—uniform the Indians wore 16 years earlier, he said, "I swore back in 1975, once that season ended, I'd never wear this red-on-red [expletive] again.

"Some people said I looked like a blood clot, and others said I looked like a giant Bloody Mary. They both were right. It was awful. Those all-red uniforms were the only thing I didn't like about playing for Frank [Robinson] in Cleveland."

Vic Power
(First baseman, 1958-1961)

Vic Power recalled the night he tied a major league record by stealing home twice in the same game against Detroit on August 14, 1958.

"We were losing and the first [stolen base] tied the game, and the second won it [9-8] in the 10th inning," he said. "A sportswriter came to me and said, 'How could you do that? You are too fat, and you are not fast. How could you do that?'

"I told him it was a night game, and nobody saw me coming. If it had been a day game, I could not have done it. They would have seen me and caught me."

It's a record that almost certainly will never be broken. As Power said, "Somebody will have to steal home three times in one game, and nobody can do that."

• • • • •

Power recalled the time that he and "Mudcat" Grant were in Cooperstown for an exhibition game with the Indians.

"We met Ty Cobb," Power said. "I had read about him, how hard he played and how hard he was on other players. He asked me how much I was hitting, and I told him '.319,' which I was very proud of. He told me, 'What's a matter, you in a slump?'

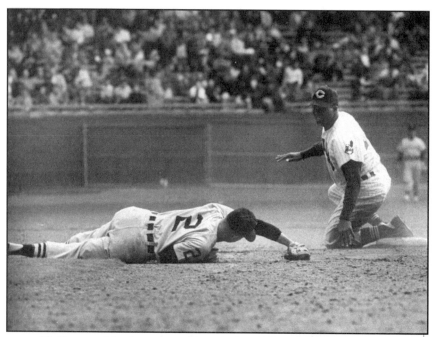

Vic Power slides into second base before White Sox Nellie Fox can make the tag. Power set a major league record for stealing home plate three times in one game. George Silk/Time Life Pictures/Getty Images

"Later I checked his record and he used to hit .380, .390, so I guess that's what he meant when he said I must have been in a slump."

Dick Radatz
(Pitcher, 1966-1967)

From 1962 to 1965, when he pitched for Boston and was the best reliever in baseball, Dick Radatz was nicknamed "The Monster" with good reason. He was six foot five, weighed 235 pounds, and had a fastball that was clocked in the high 90s, often reaching 100 mph.

But then, inexplicably, Radatz suffered, in his words, "a mental thing" and couldn't throw a strike if there was a batter at the plate.

"It was no problem warming up, but as soon as a batter stepped in against me, I couldn't throw the ball anywhere near the plate," he said.

The Indians traded for Radatz in 1966 in the hope of "rehabbing" him, as expressed by then-Tribe manager Birdie Tebbetts, but to no avail. He went 0-3 with a 4.61 earned run average in 39 appearances.

"I tried everything. I even went to a psychiatrist who hypnotized me, but that didn't help, either," Radatz lamented.

After the Indians released him early in the 1967 season, Radatz tried again to recapture the rapture he'd known previously with the Red Sox in trials with the Chicago Cubs, Detroit, and Montreal. But it was all in vain, and his career ended in 1969.

•   •   •   •   •

Of his brief tenure in Cleveland, Radatz recalled, "Gabe Paul cut my salary 25 percent, the maximum allowed, from $42,500 to less than $32,000. When I complained to Gabe, he said to me, 'Dick, you're from Detroit, aren't you?' I told him I was, and he said, 'Well, if you don't like what I'm offering, get a job on the assembly line at the Ford Motor Co.'

"I said, 'But Gabe, I'm a college graduate. I have a college degree,' and he said, 'Then get a white-collar job at Ford.'

"That's the way baseball was in those days, before Marvin Miller and free agency. Looking back at what happened then is funny now, but it wasn't funny to me at the time."

Manny Ramirez
(Outfielder, 1993-2000)

"There are so many Manny Ramirez stories. ... He is really funny, like the night we were in Oakland and he hit three consecutive home runs, each time with somebody else's bat, including mine for the third home run," Omar Vizquel recalled his former teammate.

"Three home runs with three different bats! That's an unbelievable story, but it's true."

• • • • •

During the 2003 American League Championship Series between Boston and New York, Red Sox manager Grady Little offered this opinion of the former Tribe outfielder, who left Cleveland as a free agent during the winter of 2000-2001.

"It would take longer than this interview room would allow me to tell you about Manny. He has some weird ways, but I know if each baseball fan in the country had the time and opportunity to know the kid, they would probably not be thinking too many negative thoughts about him."

• • • • •

And this Ramirez story by his former Boston team-mate Lou Merloni, a member of the Indians in 2004.

"This was [in 2003], just before our [Red Sox] starting lineup was set to run out on the field at the start of a game. Our starting pitcher was toweling off, getting ready to take the mound, and from the end of the dugout I hear, 'Let's go, guys.'

"So Manny runs out on the field, but everybody else stayed in the dugout. He went all the way to left field before he noticed that he was all alone on the field, and everybody else was still in the dugout. The fans loved it. They started cheering, and Manny tipped his cap and smiled. He got as big a kick out of it as everybody else."

Pedro Ramos
(Pitcher, 1962-1964)

It seemed that Pedro Ramos—a.k.a. "Pistol Pete"—was always under suspicion for throwing spitballs during his three seasons with the Indians, as well as previously with the Washington Senators/Minnesota Twins (1955-1961), and later with the New York Yankees, Philadelphia, Pittsburgh, Cincinnati, and Washington through 1970, when he ended a 15-year major league career.

"Pete had a pitch that he called a *Cuban palm ball*," said Doc Edwards, who not only was Ramos's catcher but also his roommate on the road.

Naturally, Edwards would not confirm that the Cuban palm ball was a spitter, although batters constantly made that accusation and often the umpires would go to the mound to check the balls Ramos threw.

"But they never found anything," Edwards said, "although one came close one night in 1962. It was veteran umpire Ed Runge, who got suspicious when several batters complained to him, and he noticed a large tobacco stain on Pete's uniform pants.

"Runge made Ramos go into the clubhouse and change, which Pete did. When he came out with clean pants and made a couple more pitches, Runge went out again and this time made Pete go in and change his jersey.

"But the same thing happened when Pete returned to the mound. Runge was still suspicious and then he ordered Pete to change his cap.

"When Ramos came back to the mound he was wearing a hard cap, a batting helmet, and all Runge could do was laugh."

Frank Robinson
(Manager–designated hitter, 1975-1977)

Prior to Frank Robinson's first spring training game as Major League Baseball's first black manager, he was asked by reporters if he was nervous.

"Not at all," he replied, then added, betraying his calmness, "although I did forget to put on my jock strap. … [That's] the first time I ever forgot to do that."

John Rocker
(Pitcher, 2001)

When John Rocker was acquired from Atlanta on June 22, 2001, in a trade for Steve Karsay and Steve Reed, then-Indians general manager John Hart predicted great success for the controversial pitcher.

"With John Rocker we're bringing in a devastating left-handed late reliever," Hart said. "[Rocker] is 26. He's a dominant closer … a workhorse who has never been on the disabled list … and has [compiled] great numbers in the regular season and the postseason."

However, it turned out to be one of the worst trades in Hart's career. In less than a full season with the Tribe, Rocker appeared in 38 games with a 3-7 won-lost record, four saves, and a 5.45 earned run average, and was traded to Texas on December 18, 2001.

•   •   •   •   •

Upon joining the Indians, Rocker was asked by reporters about the angry reaction to a 2000 *Sports Illustrated* story in which he was quoted as being highly critical of New York and New Yorkers.

"Why is reaction such a big deal to you people?" Rocker snapped to reporters. "Who cares about reaction? The mound is still 60 feet [and] six inches from home plate. There'll be a guy standing there with a 32-ounce bat. Who gives a damn about reaction?

"I sure as hell don't."

John Rocker (front) spent one season with the Indians. Although he got to celebrate the team's clinching the American League Central Division championship, he was traded to Texas three months later.
David Maxwell/AFP/Getty Images

• • • • •

Although most of his troubles concerned his erratic pitching, one day late in the season it was something else, as catcher Eddie Taubensee remembered.

"I went to the mound to talk to Rocker and to tell him that the umpire told me, 'Tell Rocker his fly is open,'" Taubensee said. "So I said, 'Hey, Rock, your fly's open,' and he said, 'Yeah, so what?'

"Well, the fans must have noticed it, too, because they really got on him that day—but I don't think it was only because they also saw that his fly was open."

Ricardo Rodriguez
(Pitcher, 2002-2003)

After Dmitri Young hit a 420-foot homer off Ricardo Rodriguez in a game against the Tigers on May 28, 2003, in Detroit, the rookie pitcher said, "I made a good pitch, and he it a long way. A real long way. All I can do is go like this," and he folded his hands and bowed his head in prayer.

Rich Rollins
(Third baseman, 1970)

"When people ask me what was my biggest thrill in baseball, I tell them, 'That's easy,'" said Rich Rollins, who grew up on the Cleveland sandlots but played most of his professional career for Minnesota.

"It was in 1962 when I was a rookie playing third base for the Twins and I was elected [then by the players] to the American League All-Star team and got more votes than any other player in either league."

Rollins batted .298 with 16 homers and drove in 96 runs for the Twins that season.

John Romano
(Catcher, 1960-1964)

"I was coming off a pretty good season in 1964 and thought I was entitled to a pretty good raise, but I had a lot of contract problems with Gabe Paul that winter [1964-1965]," John Romano said. "I'd hit .241 with 19 homers in 106 games, which was pretty good for a catcher, and I wanted more money than the $45,000 Gabe was offering.

"Finally, he called me at my home in New Jersey and told me to meet him in Cleveland, that he was going to take care of me. I figured he meant he was to settle my contract. But when I go to Cleveland, he really shocked me.

"Gabe said to me, 'Johnny, I want you to be the first to know we just traded you to the White Sox.' I was really surprised. I mean I came all the way from New Jersey to be told I was traded away ... that I wasn't getting the raise I wanted?

"When I finally recovered my voice, I said to him, 'Gabe, I want you to be the first to know that I am retiring,' and I went back home.

"A few days later Ed Short, the White Sox general manager, called and talked me into joining the White Sox—but not until he gave me the raise I was trying to get from Gabe. It was $9,000, the best raise I ever got in baseball.

"And you think times haven't changed?"

·   ·   ·   ·   ·

"I also think sometimes that if it hadn't been for me, Frank Lane would not have traded Rocky Colavito to Detroit for Harvey Kuenn [in 1960].

"Here's how I got involved. I was with the Indians then, and we were playing a spring training exhibition game in Memphis. I was sitting in the lobby of the hotel the morning of the game, and Lane came up to me and said, 'Johnny, I need to ask you something. If a game is on the line in the ninth inning and the other team has the tying run on third and the winning run on second, who would you rather pitch to, Rocky Colavito or Harvey Kuenn?

"I should have realized that something was in the works. In retrospect, Lane probably had already made up his mind to trade Rocky. He just wanted some reassurance that it was a good deal [for the Indians]. But at the time I never gave that a second thought. I just figured Lane was talking for the sake of talking, which he did a lot.

"I told him flat out that I'd rather pitch to Colavito in a spot like that. I mean, logically, if you're on the other team and had your choice, you had to pitch to Colavito because Kuenn was a much better hitter for average than

Rocky. A day or two later Lane made the trade—Colavito for Kuenn.

"This sure is a funny game sometimes."

Al Rosen
(First and third baseman, 1947-1956)

Although he was with the Indians for only the final month of the 1948 season, Al Rosen remembers that team—which won the American League pennant and beat the Boston Braves in the World Series—as "a feisty, tough bunch of guys who took nothing from nobody."

And Rosen, a former collegiate boxing champion at the University of Miami fit in perfectly then and in his eight subsequent seasons as a leader of the Tribe.

On one occasion, late in his career, Rosen made clear his unwillingness to "back down" to anybody. It took place in Yankee Stadium against the team that the Indians, in Rosen's era, always seemed to be fighting for the pennant.

A key member of the Indians claimed he couldn't play that night, complaining of a sore muscle in his leg as he lay on the trainer's table. Rosen stalked into the room and said, with sarcasm dripping from his voice, "Big men play big games."

The player on the table cursed at Rosen, and more profanity followed from both men.

Finally, Rosen said, "OK, I think it's best that you not say anything more to me, and I won't say anything more to you."

With that Rosen turned and walked to the door of the trainer's room when the other player called him a "yellow, no good son of a bitch." Rosen turned around, went back into the trainer's room, and a fight ensued. It took three men to pull them apart.

"Nobody calls me yellow," Rosen said of the fight.

How about "son of a bitch"?

"Well," he said, "that's bad enough, but don't ever call me yellow."

Few ever did—and never a second time.

And as a postscript to the fight, both players played against the Yankees that night, Rosen with a black eye and a sore fist, and the other player with a swollen jaw—and a sore leg.

●　●　●　●　●

"I switched from third base to first base in 1954 so that Al [Lopez] could play Rudy Regalado at third because he'd had a monster spring training. If Al had asked me to walk across Lake Erie, I would have tried. After I switched to first base, I broke my [right index] finger, but I didn't know until the end of the season that it was broken."

●　●　●　●　●

"I endorsed Chesterfield cigarettes [after winning the MVP award in 1953]. I don't know why I did it. I didn't even smoke. They paid me $500, but after a while I felt so guilty about it I sent the money back. But there are still pictures of me out there with a cigarette in my hand. It's very embarrassing."

Al Rosen (left) is congratulated by his Indians teammates as he runs off the field during a game against the Yankees in 1955. Ralph Morse/Time Life Pictures/Getty Images

• • • • •

"George Steinbrenner and I tried to buy the Indians from Vernon Stouffer in [November] 1971, and it's still hard to believe the way it turned out.

"It was really a shocker because we thought the deal was all sewed up. We had a truly high-powered group of investors, including Gabe Paul and F.J. "Steve" O'Neill, and some very prominent Cleveland businessmen.

"Vernon Stouffer [then the Indians owner] led us to believe that he had accepted our offer. The bare bones of the deal called for us to pay Stouffer $8.3 million, which then was a large sum for a baseball franchise, and to assume a $300,000 debt the Indians owed the television station [that broadcast their games].

"Then we got a call from Stouffer that the deal was off, that he was going to sell to Nick Mileti. It was a real shocker."

(Mileti reportedly paid Stouffer $10 million for the franchise, although Paul, then the Indians president and general manager, later called Mileti's bid "only green stamps and promises.")

C.C. Sabathia
(Pitcher, 2001-)

After winning his final game for a 17-5 won-lost record as a rookie in 2001, C.C. Sabathia said, "Those [32] starts I had before today couldn't compare to this one. I never felt like I did today. The closest I can put it is this— when I was a little kid and my mom would take me to Toys 'R Us and, you know, you get that anxious feeling because you can pick out anything you want.

"That was what the feeling was like today. I was like a kid in a candy store"—or better still, a kid in a Toys 'R Us store.

Chico Salmon and Barry Bonds demonstrate batting stances while at the Pan Am World Series in Havana, Cuba in 1984. Salmon was the manager of the Panama team and Bonds, a senior at Arizona State, played for the American team. Russell Schneider Collection

Chico Salmon
(Infielder–Outfielder, 1964-1968)

In 1966, Birdie Tebbetts, then the manager of the Indians, "nominated" Ruthford Eduardo "Chico" Salmon for the American League All-Star team.

Salmon was incredulous, even speechless—almost—when Birdie's praise was repeated. "Man, what a t'rill that would be [to make the team]," he said. "Why, I'd be the biggest man in Panama. Everyone would want to talk to me. Imagine. I'd be the first boy from Panama to make the

All-Star team. My mother would be amazed. I mean, happy. So would I. So happy I don't know what I'd do, man."

Richie Scheinblum
(Outfielder, 1965, 1967-1969)

One of the Indians' all-time favorite personalities was Richie Scheinblum, an outfielder who seemed to blush every time a reporter interviewed him or a fan asked for his autograph.

Richie compiled impressive statistics in the minor leagues but couldn't maintain his success in brief trials with the Tribe in 1965, 1967, and 1968, and after securing a place on the major league roster in 1969, primarily as a part-time outfielder–pinch hitter. In that one full season with the Indians, Scheinblum, a switch-hitter, batted .186 in 102 games, after which his contract was sold to the then-Washington Senators.

Despite his inability to hit with the same degree of consistency he enjoyed in the minors, Scheimblum never lost his youthful naïveté and enthusiasm. In his first spring training with the Tribe in 1965 he was quoted in *The Plain Dealer*: "I'm rooming with Rocky Colavito … imagine that! He's a swell fellow and I really like him. All we talk about is baseball, and it's great.

"You know, we grew up on the same neighborhood in the Bronx. Of course, Rocky is older [by nine years] than I am, but my house was right across the street from Costona Park where Rocky was first scouted by the Indians. In 1958, when I was 14 and playing around the neighborhood, Rocky was a rookie and hit 21 homers. I kept track of every one of them. And now I'm rooming with him. I still can't believe it.

"And you know what else? We both have flat feet, probably from running on the same pavement on the streets in New York. How about that?"

•   •   •   •   •

During a spring training intrasquad game in Tucson, Arizona, in 1966, Scheinblum hit a 415-foot drive over the left field wall at Hi Corbett Field. But instead of standing at the plate and admiring his handiwork, Richie put his head down and took off full speed. Early Wynn, who was coaching at first base, shouted to Richie, "Go hard ... go hard," which Scheinblum did, without looking to see where the ball went (as it soared over the fence).

Scheinblum rounded first base and headed for second, still running hard—and still with his head down—and his teammates in the Indians dugout took up the cry, "Run, Richie, run, run, run," which Richie did, still without looking to see where the ball went.

When Scheinblum approached third base, coach George Strickland waved for him to go home, which Richie did, still running hard and with his head down. The next Indians batter at the plate signaled for Scheinblum to slide, which he also did, thinking he had an inside-the-park homer. As he crossed the plate in a cloud of dust, the puzzled umpire told Scheinblum the ball had gone over the wall, that he didn't need to slide—after which Richie sat down in the dugout with his teammates and as usual blushed.

Herb Score
(Pitcher, 1955-1959)

Buddy Bell once said of Herb Score, "He's such a nice guy, I bet he makes the bed in his hotel room when he wakes up in the morning."

Despite his great ability—and outstanding record before suffering a serious eye injury in 1957—Score never took himself too seriously.

Looking back on his career, Score once said, "A lot of pitchers don't use a wind up, but I deserve credit for being the first to do so. That's because I walked so many batters and had so many runners on base so often, it seemed I was always pitching from a stretch and I almost forgot how to wind up."

• • • • •

On May 1, 1955, Score, then a rookie, pitched the nightcap of a doubleheader against Boston, after veteran Bob Feller hurled the opener. It turned out to be quite a day for the two pitchers. Feller hurled a one-hitter to win the first game, and Score struck out 16 batters in a four-hit victory in the second game.

In a first page story the next morning, *The Plain Dealer* called Feller "a fading meteor" and Score "a rising star." It reported, "26,595 fans in the Stadium had the privilege of seeing the best pitcher of this generation [Feller] and his logical successor [Score] give sparkling performances."

Richie Sexson
(First baseman and outfielder, 1997-2000)

Although he's one of the premier sluggers in the major leagues, Richie Sexson was drafted almost as an afterthought by the Indians in 1993. They picked him in the 24th round after more than 700 players had been taken.

So how does a 24th-round draft choice not only get to the major leagues, but also become one of the most prolific home run hitters? It was Sexson's will to succeed.

"I never worried about what round the Indians drafted me or how many players were picked ahead of me. It was no big deal. I knew I was drafted pretty late, but I knew what I wanted to accomplish—that I wanted to do this, play in the big leagues. I guess it was a matter of will. All I ever wanted to do was play professional baseball, and when you love the game and put a lot of preparation into it, good things can happen."

Sonny Siebert
(Pitcher, 1964-1969)

"The Indians always had the best fastball-pitching staff in baseball, back in the 1960s, and I'll tell you the reason why," Sonny Siebert said. "It was all because of Birdie Tebbetts. You didn't pitch for Birdie unless you could throw hard. When he was the manager the Indians, they didn't even sign a pitcher unless he could throw the heck out of the ball."

Which Siebert could, as did his starting pitching partners of that era: Sam McDowell, Luis Tiant, and Steve Hargan.

Duke Sims
(Catcher, 1964-1970)

"My lifetime batting average was only .239 due to one of the most inept official scorers of all time," complained Duke Sims, whose memory obviously was much better than his batting eye. "It should be .240, not .239, because I was screwed out of a hit in 1968 on a ball that was ruled an error [charged to New York Yankees second baseman Horace Clarke].

"Because of that my career average [for 11 years in the major leagues] was .2394 and was rounded off—*down*—to .239. But if I had gotten credit for that hit, as I should have, my average would have been .2398, and would have been rounded off—*up*—to .240.

"Here's how it happened. We were playing the Yankees at the [old] Stadium and [southpaw] Steve Barber was on the mound for them. Now, being a left-handed batter, I seldom faced left-handed pitchers, especially not those who ate up left-handed batters the way Barber did. He was one of the nastiest left handers in the league. He had nasty, nasty stuff, but Alvin Dark left me in to face him for some reason—maybe because Joe Azcue was hurt or sleeping or something.

"Well, Barber threw me a sidearm low, inside fastball that I crushed. I really did, believe me. I hit it right at Clarke, and it handcuffed him [and] went through his legs, and after long deliberation, the official scorer called it an error. An error! I couldn't believe it. Neither could Clarke. I argued with the scorer after the game, and all he said to me was, 'That was an easy play for a major league infielder.' I asked him, 'Does that mean Horace Clarke is not a major leaguer?'

"And because it was called an error, I wound up with one less hit [580] in my career [in 2,422 official at-bats for an 11-season batting average of .2394715]. If I had been credited with a hit, my average would have been .2398 [.2398843] and would have been rounded off to .240."

(Author's note: The "inept scorer" to whom Sims referred was Russell Schneider—yes, the author of this book—and states here that the play was called correctly. It was not a hit; it was an error because major league second basemen are supposed to make that kind of play.)

When asked if the Indians won or lost the game in which Sims was "screwed" by the "inept scorer," his memory failed him.

• • • • •

Something else Sims recalled from his seven-year career with the Indians was a plan he crafted in 1968 to try to force then-general manager Gabe Paul to give him and fellow catcher Joe Azcue big raises in 1968. Sims wanted Azcue to join him in holding out as a tandem, as Don Drysdale and Sandy Koufax did to the Los Angeles Dodgers in 1965.

"I told Joe that our position, catcher, was worth $100,000, because Johnny Bench had just signed with Cincinnati for 100 grand," Sims said. "I said to Joe, 'Let's hold out together, because the Indians needed either one of us and couldn't do without both of us. Each of us will get $50,000, but if Gabe negotiates with us individually, he'll break us apart and say that neither of us is worth $50,000.'

"The way I had it figured, Bench was the Cadillac catcher of both leagues, and not only that, Bill Freehan was making about $80,000 in Detroit. My rationale was simple—the [catching] position is worth $100,000, in our case, $50,000 for each of us.

"At the time I was making about $16,000 and Joe was making probably $25,000. So I figured it, Gabe had about 60 grand on the table for the position and our combined numbers, Joe's and mine, were better than Bench's. It made sense for the two of us combined to get at least as much as Bench. The Indians were not going to let either Joe or me go to the plate 600 times, but together we would.

"Something else. Remember that a catcher works twice as hard as any other guy on the field—runs the defense, runs the pitching staff, and in order to be properly rewarded [with money] he has to be an offensive player, too. You could be a great catcher but never make any big money—not in my day anyway. In our case, Joe [a right-handed batter] faced all the nasty-ass left handers and I [a left-handed batter] got all the toughest right-handed pitchers in baseball.

"But Joe said, 'Oh, roomie, I got two kids and [the Indians] might release me. I cannot take that chance,' and wouldn't go along with me. But I held out anyway, though it didn't do me much good. I wound up getting something like $18,000 or $19,000. Joe never did tell me what he got."

Grady Sizemore
(Outfielder, 2004-)

How good a prospect did the Indians consider Grady Sizemore to be when he played—and starred—at Class AA Akron in 2003 and Class AAA Buffalo in 2004?

Teammate Corey Smith might have said it best: "When Grady rolls out of bed, he hits line drives. He is amazing."

And as Tribe director of player development John Farrell said, "He has the potential with his tremendous ability and work ethic to be a team leader and become a star-caliber player at the big league level."

Joel Skinner
(Catcher, 1989-1991; coach, 2001-; interim manager, 2002)

After replacing fired manager Charlie Manuel in July 2002, Joel Skinner led the Indians to a 35-41 record. When the season ended, he was considered a frontrunner for the full-time job based on comments by general manager Mark Shapiro.

When asked to assess Skinner's assets, Shapiro listed them as "patience, positiveness, and his appreciation of the Cleveland Indians organization."

"I think he managed a game extremely well," Shapiro said.

A week later Shapiro signed Eric Wedge to a two-year contract to manage the Indians.

Shane Spencer
(Outfielder, 2003)

"When I was with the Yankees [1998-2002] and we came to Jacobs Field for the 1998 playoffs, my dad came up to see a game," Shane Spencer recalled. "When I got back to the hotel after the game and my dad wasn't around, I asked my friends if they knew where he went, and they told me he went out with some Cleveland fans. Later he told me that the fans told him, 'We like your son, but we hate the Yankees.'"

Charlie Spikes
(Outfielder, 1973-1977)

As a No. 1 draft choice of the New York Yankees in 1969, great things were expected of Charlie Spikes when he was acquired by the Indians in 1973 in a trade that sent Graig Nettles to New York.

Nicknamed the "Bogalusa Bomber" (his home was in Bogalusa, Louisiana), Spikes hammered 23 homers and drove in 73 runs although he batted only .237 in 140 games his first season in Cleveland. His numbers improved in 1974—.271 average, 22 homers, 80 RBIs—but in 1975, with the arrival of Frank Robinson as baseball's first black manager, Spikes's career took a nose-dive.

"A lot of people were critical of Frank, saying that he put too much pressure on me, but it was my own fault, not his," Spikes said. "Everybody has differences of opinion, and Frank and I did, too. Let me say it this way. I was trying so hard to do well because I wanted Frank to do well as the first black manager.

"But I got off to a bad start. I went zero for 21, and Frank benched me. When I got back in the lineup, if I didn't hit well, he'd take me out again. But I don't blame Frank. That was me, my fault, not Frank's. I put pressure on myself. Frank didn't do it."

• • • • •

Spikes suffered a back injury a few years ago, underwent two operations, and was forced to give up his job in a textile factory in Louisiana.

"Nobody calls me the 'Bogalusa Bomber' anymore," he said.

Now they call him "Charles Leslie Spikes"—when he signs for his disability insurance.

Scott Stewart
(Pitcher, 2004)

Southpaw pitcher Scott Stewart said he knew he'd be booed when he was introduced for the Indians' home opener because of the poor record he compiled in spring training. He took it in stride, even tipping his cap to the fans as he took his place alongside teammates on the third base line.

"It was a respectable boo," he said. "Besides, I've heard worse, [and] it's better to be booed than spit upon."

A month into the season, with his won lost record an abysmal 0-2 and with a 7.24 earned run average in 23 appearances—and the fans still booing—Stewart was designated for assignment and sent to Class AAA Buffalo.

George Strickland
(Shortstop, 1952-1957, 1959-60;
coach, 1963-1969; interim manager, 1964, 1966)

"[The 1960s] were difficult times in Cleveland," George Strickland remembered. "There was so much politics involved, and there always seemed to be money problems. [Owner] Vernon Stouffer had pretty much put Alvin Dark in complete control of the club [in 1969], and it sometimes got to be very difficult.

"But when you check out the records of the pitchers we had then—Sam McDowell, Luis Tiant, Sonny Siebert, Steve Hargan, and some others—you have to wonder why we, the Indians, didn't do better. I guess it was because they were all too young then and became great pitchers after they left the Indians, which was a shame."

• • • • •

"If somebody had asked me when I was managing the Indians, 'Who had the best fastball in baseball?' I would have said, 'Sam McDowell.'

"And if I was asked, 'Who had the best curveball?' I would have said, 'McDowell.'

"'How about the best change-up?' It also would have been McDowell.

"'The best slider?' Again, McDowell."

So why didn't McDowell do better, regardless of his drinking problem?

"I honestly believe that Sam was afraid of success," Strickland said.

• • • • •

Strickland—a slick-fielding, light-hitting shortstop—played for the Indians after being acquired from Pittsburgh in 1952.

"I was glad to go to Cleveland, which had a very good team then under Al Lopez, and I didn't mind leaving the Pirates, who were very bad then.

"We were so bad [in Pittsburgh] I think we were the only team in the history of baseball to be mathematically eliminated [from the pennant race] by June."

• • • • •

In 1954, when the Indians were in the process of winning a then-American League-record 111 games, Strickland was lost for six weeks after suffering a broken jaw when he was hit by a thrown ball while sliding into third base against the Yankees in New York on July 23.

Although the injury was serious—Strickland's jaw was wired shut for more than a month—there was a humorous aspect to the incident.

"One of the reporters [Jim Schlemmer of the *Akron Beacon Journal*] wrote that he had never seen courage like I showed that night, crawling to get to the base after I got hit," Strickland said, chuckling as he recounted the story by phone from his home in New Orleans. "When I read what Schlemmer wrote, I told him through my clenched teeth, 'Thanks for the kind words, and I hate to blow your story. But the truth is, I wasn't trying to get back to the base, … I was just trying to find my denture.'

George Strickland relaxes after a game in 1959. George Silk/Time Life Pictures/Getty Images

"Schlemmer told me, 'Well, don't say anything about it because everybody liked the story the way I wrote it, and I did, too.'

"I loved Jim. He was a fraud. He wanted people to think he was a nasty guy, a tough guy, but he was a real pussycat. It's like I always said, 'It's hard to meet bad people in baseball.' At least it was when I was up there.

"I was playing second base the night that Herb [Score] got hit by the liner off the bat of Gil McDougald. That was as bad as I ever saw. It happened so quickly. I ran to the mound, and Herb turned his head and all of a sudden he was bleeding from everywhere. His eyes, his nose, his mouth, his ears, everywhere. It was awful. Probably the thing that saved him was that the ball hit the side of his nose first. If it had gone right into the eye, it would have been worse. Very bad."

• • • • •

And when Strickland retired, he said, "I knew it was time to go when the players started bringing hair driers to the clubhouse, and you'd get on a team bus and eight or 10 guys would be carrying those boomboxes, and all of them tuned to something different."

Brian Tallet
(Pitcher, 2002-)

In 2003, when southpaw Brian Tallet was trying to make the team—before he was sidelined for the season with an arm injury that required major surgery—he realized he was in trouble during a game he was pitching for Class AAA Buffalo.

Catcher Josh Bard went to the mound and said to Tallet, "Dude, I called for a fastball."

"That's what I threw," Tallet retorted.

"Dude, it was 81 [miles per hour]."

A month later Tallet underwent a "Tommy John" elbow operation, ulnar nerve transposition, and removal of bone chips and bone spurs.

Jim Thome
(First and third baseman, 1991-2002)

When Jim Thome became a free agent at the end of the 2002 season, he received and eventually accepted a six-year $85 million offer from the Philadelphia Phillies.

However, before he signed with the Phillies, Thome met one more time with the Indians, who were offering him $63.25 million over five years to remain in Cleveland.

Of his negotiations with Tribe general manager Mark Shapiro, Thome said, "I called [Shapiro] up, and I said, 'Mark, if you will guarantee me a sixth year at the same money [$63.25 million] you're offering, I'll take it. I'm not asking for any more money, just one more year at the same amount you're willing to pay me for five. If you will, I'll sign this thing right now and get it over with.'

"[Shapiro] said he couldn't ... but never explained why, except to tell me, 'My hands are tied.' Don't ask me what he meant by that. But that was it for me. The end [of negotiations with the Indians]."

Robby Thompson
(Coach, 2002)

Talking about his playing career (1986-1996) with the San Francisco Giants, whose then-general manager was former Indians third baseman Al Rosen: "One time [in 1989] after an important game, I told Al, 'You were the most red-assed general manager I ever saw. From my position at second base, I could see into your box. When we made a costly error, you'd go berserk. Once I saw you rip the phone out of your box and throw it. After we lost a game through inept play, you came into the clubhouse and told manager Roger Craig to call a meeting, and you gave us such a chewing out I still can't forget it. You ripped our butts, the greatest chewing out I ever heard.'"

Luis Tiant
(Pitcher, 1964-1969)

When he was in his prime with the Indians in the late 1960s, Luis Tiant had a "corkscrew" windup/delivery that entertained fans as much as it confused batters.

"I didn't do it for show," Tiant said. "I did it to get batters out. They would say, 'We can't tell where the ball is coming from,' which is what I wanted them to worry about. I gave [the batters] my shoulder, back, foot, and—finally—the ball."

Tiant also talked a lot to hitters he was facing.

"I'd tell them, 'Hit this one, if you can.'"

Most of the time they couldn't.

• • • • •

When Tiant joined the Indians as a rookie in 1964, one of his teammates was third baseman–outfielder Al Smith, who said he had played against Tiant's father, Luis Sr., in the Negro League in 1946 and 1947.

"If this kid is half as good as his father, we've got us a helluva pitcher," Smith said.

Indeed, Tiant proved to be more than "half as good" as his father had been, and it turned out that the Indians did have a helluva pitcher.

Luis Jr. went 10-4 as a rookie and in 1968 led the American League with a 1.60 earned run average with a 21-9 won-lost record.

• • • • •

"I pitched for Los Angeles [1958-1962] when the Dodgers had [Don] Drysdale and [Sandy] Koufax and for the New York Yankees [1963-1964] when they had [Ralph] Terry and [Mel] Stottlemyre before I came to Cleveland," said Stan Williams, who pitched for Cleveland in 1965 and from 1967 to 1969, "and in my opinion Luis Tiant probably was the greatest right-handed pitcher I ever played with.

"Not only was he a great pitcher and a great competitor, Looie also was one of the funniest men I've ever known. He kept everybody loose with his antics—like, he'd smoke a big cigar in the shower, run around the clubhouse naked, swing from the overhead pipes like a big gorilla, crazy things like that.

"One of the funny things that I remember so well is what he did to our first baseman, Tony Horton, a big, six-foot-four strapping guy—and a very serious guy. Steve Hamilton, he of the famous 'blooper'—or what he called his 'eephus' pitch—was on the mound for the Yankees and threw his blooper to Horton during a game in 1968. Tony took a vicious swing at the ball and popped it up to the third baseman, who'd been playing deep and had to charge in and dive to catch it.

"When it happened, Tiant ran out of the dugout and—in front of all the crowd—put his finger under Horton's chin like it was a fish hook and literally dragged Tony back to the dugout."

Omar Vizquel
(Shortstop, 1994-2004)

"There are so many things that happen during your career, you could write a book about it," Omar Vizquel said. "One of them was the time I made three errors in one game [in 1994], which I never had done before and haven't done since. I never thought I would have a game like that. The fans started screaming names at me, saying what are you doing here and why didn't I stay in Seattle—instead of being traded here—things like that.

"I knew I had to do something to try to get the fans back on my side and to regain the confidence of my teammates. So I went the next two months without making an error, something like that, and everything was forgotten. I finished the season with only eight errors and won my first [of nine consecutive] Gold Gloves."

Omar Vizquel leaps out of the way of Detroit's Bobby Higgenson after tagging Higgenson and making the throw to first base to complete the double play. AP/WWP

•   •   •   •   •

"So many funny things also happen in a player's career. Like the time we were losing 12-2 [to Seattle in 2001] and came back to win. Charlie Manuel came to me in the fifth inning when we were still down by six or seven runs and said, 'Be ready because you are going to be the hero of this game.'

"I came up in the ninth inning with the bases loaded and hit a triple to tie the game and we went on to win.

"Stuff like that. Sometimes it's hard to believe."

•   •   •   •   •

"Another time I was fielding a ground ball, and it rolled up my arm to my chin and went down inside my shirt. The runner just kept running, and all I could do was hug him because I couldn't get my hand on the ball. Everybody started yelling, and at first the umpire didn't know what to call although he finally called the guy safe because I couldn't tag him—the ball was still inside my shirt."

•   •   •   •   •

When coach Buddy Bell was asked to rate Vizquel as a shortstop, he said, "If Ozzie Smith is in the Hall of Fame, Omar has to make it, too. I've seen them both a lot. Ozzie was more flamboyant, but if you put a gun against my head, I'd have to say Omar is better overall. He's the smartest player I've ever been around."

And this praise for Vizquel from another outstanding shortstop–third baseman, Alex Rodriguez of the New York Yankees, "[Omar] is a phenomenal defensive player. He's like an artist. It's fun to watch all the defensive styles, and his is the most unique. All the barehanded plays he makes.

"He's an innovator."

Eric Wedge
(Manager, 2003-)

How anxious was Eric Wedge to start his career as a major league manager?

"After getting the job [on October 29, 2002], I was very excited. [I] spent the winter in Cleveland preparing for everything and decided to drive down to Winter Haven, [Florida], with my [new] wife, Kate."

They were married November 16, 2002.

"Winter Haven is about a 17-hour drive from Cleveland, and we planned to go halfway and stop en route at least one night. But once I started driving, my mind got to working and I got to thinking about spring training and how excited I was to get it going. The next thing I knew we were 10 hours, 11 hours, 13 hours on the road and were getting to the point where it was almost too close to stop—so we didn't.

"We ended up driving all day and through the night … all the way straight to Winter Haven in a little more than 16 hours. That was February 9 and 10, and although spring training didn't start for another week, I didn't think anything of it. I felt good and just wanted to get started. There probably were about a million different thoughts that popped through my head.

"After we arrived, [general manager] Mark Shapiro asked me where we stopped, and I told him we didn't. I thought he might scold me, but he didn't. He just laughed. A few other guys joked with me about it but it just seemed like the thing to do. I wanted to get down here. I wanted to get started."

• • • • •

What was the biggest thing Wedge learned in his rookie season as a major league manager?

"[That] it's always harder *not* to say something than it is to say something," he replied.

And, when asked to comment on the early-season hitting problems of first baseman Travis Hafner, Wedge said—in what could be construed as "Stengelese"—that Hafner "needs a consistent approach to be consistent. That's where his inconsistencies lie."

Fred Weisman
(Eldest son of Lefty Weisman,
the Indians' trainer from 1921-1949)

"I used to play the piano for my dad, who loved to sing, especially Irish songs," said Fred Weisman, now a prominent attorney in Cleveland. "Dad had a pretty good voice and so did Joe Shaute [who pitched for the Indians from 1922 to 1930]. They would harmonize together and were really good, especially Shaute, who was a great tenor. In fact, he sang the national anthem a few times before games during his career with the Indians. He and my dad used to do a little barbershop, that kind of stuff.

"Another one who had an excellent voice, and who also loved to sing, was Jim Hegan [a Tribe catcher from 1941-1942 and 1946-1957]. Hegan and a friend of his, a priest from Lynn, Massachusetts, came over to the house a lot, and they'd sing with dad while I played the piano.

"In 1946 when the Indians celebrated my dad's 25th anniversary as the team trainer, my dad sang at the Stadium before the game that night, and [owner] Bill Veeck hired a trio that backed him up. Dad loved it. So did the fans.

"I can't imagine something like that happening today. But then, times were a lot different then. I guess everything was."

Jed Weisman
(Youngest son of Lefty Weisman)

"One of the things I remember so well about the time my dad was the Indians trainer is that a lot of the players were always coming over to our house to visit, especially Jim Hegan, Joe Gordon, and Ken Keltner," said Jed Weisman, who's also a Cleveland attorney.

"In those days most of the games were played in the daytime, and the guys would come over, munch on the chopped liver my mom made, and have a few beers with my dad. Hegan didn't drink much, but Gordon and Keltner could put it away pretty good.

"It was really funny. Everybody in our neighborhood grew up knowing that somebody from the Indians would be coming over from time to time, and all the kids wondered, 'Who's going to be there tonight?' It was always a thrill for them. They'd come over for autographs, and I'm sure they envied my brother and me, but it was no big thing to us. It was always fun.

"I also got to know Earl Averill pretty well. He was one of the nicest guys in the world but acted real tough in the clubhouse. He'd grab me, put me on the rubbing table in the trainer's room, pick up my dad's scissors, and threaten to cut my ears off. He scared the hell out of me the first time he did it, which probably was the reason he continued to do it. But I liked him a lot. I liked all the guys, but Averill probably was my favorite."

Jake Westbrook
(Pitcher, 2001-)

"A lot of people expected me to be disappointed when I was traded here by the Yankees, but I wasn't, not in the least," Jake Westbrook said. "It wasn't anything new, not to me, anyway. I was traded a couple of times before the Indians got me, and I always knew that trades are part of baseball, the way the game is played, which I should know as well as anybody. I was drafted by Colorado in 1996, was traded to Montreal after the 1997 season, and dealt to the Yankees after the 1999 season before I came to the Indians."

(Westbrook was acquired with pitcher Zach Day to complete a July 25, 2000, deal for David Justice.)

"Actually, nobody likes to be traded, because it tends to make you feel unwanted, but I knew that coming to the Indians would be a good opportunity for me. Besides, I didn't feel I had a real good chance to do much with the Yankees and that it would better for me here, which it was—and is."

William Wilder
(Team physician–medical director, 1970-2000; medical consultant, 2001-)

"There are a million Bert Blyleven stories, a lot of which can't be told, but one I can tell you goes back to the early 1980s, and we were giving the players their pre-spring training physicals," Dr. William Wilder said. "I still get on Bert about it when he comes in with the Twins [as a broadcaster]—and he never lets me forget it either. It was about the time I gave him a prostate exam, you know, the digital rectal exam.

"That night in Tucson, after I'd finished the physicals, my wife and I were going out for dinner. Pete Franklin, the broadcaster, was there in the lobby of the hotel doing his radio show and was interviewing Blyleven.

"When Bert saw me he said to Pete—on the air and heard by 38 states and half of Canada—'Oh, here comes Doc Wilder. He just gave us our physicals today.' Pete said, 'How'd it go?' and Bert said, 'Fine, the doctor checked my prostate, but something I don't understand—he had both of his hands on my shoulders.' Pete just about died and finally said, 'We're going to take a break.'"

• • • • •

"There also is a good Gaylord Perry story. One night he got hit in the left shin with a line drive and had to be taken out of the game. I went into the clubhouse and asked him where it hurt. He put his hand on his right leg and said, 'Here and here and here,' but every time I poked around it didn't seem to bother him no matter what I did.

"Well, he let me go through it all—his shin, his ankle, his knee, everything—and finally I said, 'Gaylord, it looks pretty good,' and he said, 'Doc, you're poking around the wrong leg.' That was Gaylord; he loved to bait me like that.

"And, on that subject, I have to say I certainly agree with what [late trainer] Jimmy Warfield always said, that Gaylord had the greatest pain tolerance of any player he ever worked on. Gaylord was famous—or maybe that should be infamous—for the hot stuff Jimmy used on Gaylord before a game. It was so hot Jimmy wore rubber gloves when he massaged Gaylord's shoulder. None of the other players could stand it.

"But Gaylord, you've got to give it to him, had his own routine, his own set of exercises, everything. He always did his own thing, never mind anyone else, and it worked. He's in the Hall of Fame, isn't he?"

(Perry was inducted into the Hall of Fame in 1991.)

Stan Williams
(Pitcher, 1965, 1967-1969)

"In 1968, when Alvin Dark managed the Indians, on two occasions he brought me in with the bases loaded, two outs and a three-and-two count on the hitter," Stan Williams remembered. "The second time he did it, after he gave me the ball and started to walk back to the dugout, I called him back to the mound and asked him, 'Skip, how do you want me to pitch to this guy?'

"He just looked at me and said, 'I don't care. Just get him out,' which I did and says a lot for our pitching strategy back then, compared to all the fancy stuff everybody in the game likes to talk about now."

Early Wynn
(Pitcher, 1949-1957, 1963; coach, 1964-1966)

Early Wynn, nicknamed "Burly Early" and renowned for his gruff demeanor and tough style of pitching, once was asked if it were true that he was so competitive he'd throw a high, hard fastball at his own mother if she were batting against him.

Wynn replied, "It would depend on how well she was hitting."

A former teammate who could testify as to Wynn's temperament was George Strickland, the Tribe shortstop from 1952 to 1957 and 1959 to 1960.

"The first game I ever played behind Early Wynn, he was having some minor problems—minor because he never had big problems. I looked into the dugout, and [manager] Al Lopez motioned for me to go over and talk to Early, to settle him down or whatever," Strickland recalled.

"I called time, walked toward the mound, and before I got halfway Early turned, glared at me, and said, 'Where the hell do you think you're going? Just turn around and get your ass back to your position and don't bother me.'

"So I did, and when I looked in the dugout again, there was Lopez and a couple of guys laughing. He set me up good. Boy, did he ever."

•   •   •   •   •

Speaking of the Tribe's 1954 pitching staff that many—Al Lopez included—consider to have been the best in baseball history, Lopez said, "The only guy who gave me trouble when I went to take him out of a game was Wynn. He'd really get upset when he was having a bad game, although he didn't have many of them.

"Once when I went out to get him, which was my second trip to the mound that inning and meant I had to bring in a relief pitcher, Early was arguing with the umpire, Bill Summers. Early must have been giving him a bad time, because just as I got there, I heard Summers tell him, 'One more word out of you and you're gone.'

"Early looked at Summers, then at me, and asked the umpire, 'Why the hell do you think [Lopez] is coming out here—to bring me a ham sandwich?'"

•   •   •   •   •

Of the Indians pitching staff of 1954, when he and Bob Lemon led the American League with 23 victories each (and Mike Garcia won 19, Art Houtteman 15, Bob Feller 13, and relievers Don Mossi, Ray Narleski, and Hal Newhouser combined to win 16), Wynn said, "I don't know for sure if we were the best staff ever, but give it to me and I'll take my chances against any other team in history."